Equity and Royalty Agreements
For Business Assistance Programs

By Nanette Kalis

National Business Incubation Association
Athens, Ohio

Copyright ©1997 by National Business Incubation Association. All rights reserved.

Printed in the United States of America.

Reproduction or translation of any part of this work beyond that permitted by Section 107 or 108 of the 1976 United States Copyright Act without the permission of the copyright owner is unlawful. Requests for permission or further information should be addressed to the Permission Department, NBIA, 20 East Circle Drive, Suite 190, Athens, Ohio 45701.

ISBN: 1-887183-41-8

National Business Incubation Association
20 East Circle Drive
Suite 190
Athens, Ohio 45701

http://www.nbia.org

Contributors

Larry Albertson, President
North Florida Technology Innovation
Corporation
Gainesville, Florida

Rich Bendis, President
Kansas Technology Enterprise Corporation
Topeka, Kansas

Dallas Breamer, Manager
Tri-Cities Enterprise Association
Richland, Washington

Janet Buehler, Partner
Metro-New York Not-For-Profit Tax Services
Coopers & Lybrand L.L.P.
New York, New York

David Day, Interim Director
University of Alabama Research Foundation
Birmingham, Alabama

Wilson Harrison, Director
Office for the Advancement of Developing
Industries
Birmingham, Alabama

Harlan Jacobs, President
Genesis Business Centers Ltd.
Columbia Heights, Minnesota

Jerry Donahue, Executive Director
Boulder Technology Incubator
Longmont and Boulder, Colorado

Bob Meeder, President
SPEDD Inc.
Wexford, Pennsylvania

Sam Pruett, Director
GENESIS Technology Incubator
University of Arkansas
Fayetteville, Arkansas

Mark Rice, Director
Center for Technological Entrepreneurship
Rensselaer Polytechnic Institute
Troy, New York

Table of Contents

Introduction		1
Chapter 1	Making the Most of Equity and Royalty Agreements	4
Chapter 2	Steps to Success	7
	Case Study: Putting a Service Plan into Action	13
Chapter 3	Structuring the Deal	16
	An Incentive Plan for Distributing Equity	25
Chapter 4	Drafting the Contract	26
Chapter 5	Equity and Royalty in University Settings	30
	Case Study: Clashing Over Equity	33
Summary		37
Appendices		38
Index		91

Introduction

Business incubation focuses a network of assistance on promising young companies of all sorts. Business incubator management diagnoses a company's needs and develops a tailored array of business assistance services delivered by staff and resource professionals who work with the incubator. Incubation programs differ in how their fees are structured. An increasing number are instituting equity and royalty arrangements as one way to benefit both companies and the programs themselves.

On the balance books, equity and royalty arrangements between business incubators or other business assistance programs and their clients make sound fiscal sense. For the incubator, these agreements represent a source of funds independent of rents, subsidies, and income from services. For young companies, they provide a way to conserve cash by trading future revenues or a percentage of sales for incubator services they need now.

Taking equity in a client company involves obtaining part ownership of the company or drawing up a stock warrant agreement that gives the business incubator the option for part ownership in the future. An equity agreement can also state that the company or any of its future strategic partners can buy out the incubator's equity position or, conversely, give the incubator stock in the company that buys out the incubator client.

Either way, the deal represents immediate savings for clients. "They can use their stock as an alternative currency and save their capital for other things that are crucial to the business," says Harlan Jacobs, president of the for-profit Genesis Business Center in Columbia Heights, Minnesota. Jacobs notes that clients also benefit because when an incubator has a stake in its companies, it wants to do everything it can to make them successful.

Generally, the amount of equity the incubator acquires ranges from 1 percent to 10 percent, with between 2 percent and 5 percent being most common. Dallas Breamer of the Tri-Cities Enterprise Association (TEA) in Richland, Washington, keeps TEA's equity position under 10 percent. Breamer, who oversees TEA's microequity fund, says, "We don't take a big piece of the company, so future funding sources won't look at us as threatening."

The incubator's equity position is usually not fixed for all companies; rather, it is negotiated on a case-by-case basis with the client. The percentage agreed upon depends on the valuation of the company and the value of services the incubator agrees to offer the client in exchange for equity. (For an exception, see University of Maryland's Technology Advancement Program [TAP] in Chapter 4.)

Although the equity percentage may vary from client to client, income from equity is always deferred. The incubator gives its services now with the understanding that it will receive cash down the line when the company goes public or is acquired by a third party. This usually takes five years or longer. The wait can often be reduced by including provisions to liquidate the incubator's equity shares in a variety of ways. For instance, if the company reaches a particular benchmark, such as obtaining venture capital, the incubator may have the option of selling its shares back to the company.

By and large, however, the incubator retains its equity in the company until a public offering or third-party acquisition occurs. For this reason, equity deals generally work best with high-growth companies, which have a better track record for selling up or going public than other companies. Royalty agreements, on the other hand, are well suited for a variety of firms, including slower-growth companies. For a royalty arrangement to prove fruitful, a company need not sell out or go on the stock market; it simply must generate gross sales.

In royalty arrangements, the business incubation program does not become a stockholder in the company. Instead, the incubator gets a percentage of either the company's sales or of income generated from a defined intellectual property owned by the company, such as a patent. Royalty commissions average between 2 percent and 5 percent of sales, and — like equity agreements — are usually negotiated on a case-by-case basis with the client.

A royalty contract provides earlier benefits to the business incubation program than an equity arrangement. The contract spells out a timeframe for royalty payments to begin and end. Most incubators allow a "start-up" period of between one and three years before payments become due. Time frames are usually expressed in dollars (for example, beginning after the first $500,000 in sales and continuing through the first $10 million in sales) or in years (for example, beginning in the company's third year and continuing through its eighth). Payments may be quarterly, though some are monthly. In some cases, sliding scales are negotiated, with royalty payments being lower in early years and increasing as the company's sales gain momentum.

More and more incubation programs have developed creative ways to utilize equity and royalty agreements, either separately or together. Over time, they have streamlined the process and learned from their mistakes. This book was created from the collective advice of these professionals and others involved in successful equity and royalty programs.

Chapter 1
Making the Most of Equity and Royalty Agreements

For equity and royalty agreements to work in business assistance programs that cater to emerging companies, both sides must gain something tangible. Those benefits must fit into an appropriate time frame and come at a reasonable "cost."

Determining if Equity or Royalty Agreements Are Right for a Program

From the incubator's point of view, the benefits of equity and royalty arrangements are impressive. The money generated can go a long way toward reaching the all-important goal of self-sufficiency. However, those who have entered into such deals with clients caution that not every incubator is suited for equity or royalty arrangements. The best-suited incubators are able to:

• **Offer high-quality services.** This is an important point, as only the most naive of entrepreneurs would agree to give up equity or royalty in exchange for run-of-the-mill services. "We do hundreds of hours of work [for equity and royalty clients] — far beyond what the normal incubator service is," says Bob Meeder, president of SPEDD, the nation's largest incubator network.

• **Choose from a solid pool of clients.** Not all clients must be multimillion-dollar winners for equity or royalty deals to work but they should be able to generate enough revenue to make worthwhile the time and effort it takes to guide them. "Focus your resources on the most promising companies," advises Mark Rice, director of the Center for Technological Entrepreneurship at Rensselaer Polytechnic Institute, Troy, New York.

• **Monitor clients' and graduates' progress on a regular basis.** Often, the equity or royalty agreement will continue even after the client has graduated. For this reason, the incubator must have the resources to oversee the company's progress, including reviewing financial statements and market strategies, on a long-term basis.

- **Link clients with potential investors and experts knowledgeable in the clients' services or products.** Many of the incubators that are involved in royalty or equity deals have a database of experts, ranging from college professors to CEOs of major corporations, who are willing to become involved with the fledgling companies. In addition, the incubators have established networks of angel investors or venture capitalists. "We not only introduce them to [potential investors]," says Jacobs of Genesis. "We groom them and train them to meet investors."

- **Balance the needs of clients.** "[Otherwise] you may be perceived as doing more for one company than another because you have a higher stake in the first company," says Sam Pruett, director of the GENESIS Technology Incubator at the University of Arkansas, Fayetteville.

Determining if an Equity or Royalty Arrangement Is Right for a Company

For the client, an equity or royalty agreement can be extremely beneficial, because such financing arrangements allow the client to conserve precious resources during the crucial early stages of development. In addition, such arrangements allow the clients to:

- **Prove that their companies have real value.** Because equity and royalty arrangements basically represent a first round of financing, clients can later approach outside investors and show that their companies have real worth. The incubator's willingness to enter into an equity or royalty agreement with the client may be the catalyst that persuades an investor to back the company. A decade ago, the role of initial investor might have been played in part by venture capitalists, but now that elite class of investors is rarely interested in financing stakes of less than a half million dollars.

- **Obtain a level of services beyond the incubator norm.** As Meeder mentioned earlier, SPEDD devotes far more time to its select equity and royalty clients than to regular clients, which reflects the fact that SPEDD is more of a partner than an advisor in the company. Other incubators follow this approach as well. The Boulder Technology Incubator, for instance, sets up an advisory board for each equity client, regardless of the client's experience. The client and board are required to meet on a monthly basis to review the company's progress and to plot strategy. In addition to grooming the client for future rounds of investment, BTI links the client to its angel capital network. The number of hours devoted to regular incubator services, such as drafting and maintaining a business plan or developing a marketing strategy, exceeds the normal incubator/client relationship.

Jacobs says it's in the best interest of both parties to make certain clients are getting the best service possible. He's getting stock in return, and "[I] want those 10,000 shares to be worth something," he says.

- **Enter the marketplace free of debt.** Breamer of TEA points out that an equity or royalty arrangement allows companies to get operating capital "without looking like they're in debt." This, in turn, is another impressive point with future investors.

Things to Consider

Not every company warms to equity or royalty arrangements. According to Rice, "A sharp entrepreneur, in my view, is going to find some way to get (comparable incubator services) without giving up equity." He adds that some venture capitalists feel the same way — "highly suspicious" of an entrepreneur who was willing to give up equity at an early stage.

For incubators, the drawbacks of equity and royalty agreements may well be worth the risk and the wait. The incubator may ultimately be able to enjoy several hundred thousands of dollars of income from these agreements if many of the companies succeed. However, if most of the companies fail, the incubator may have nothing more to show than "colorful pieces of wallpaper," as Jacobs of Genesis says of the stock certificates that an incubator obtains from its companies in equity agreements. Still, Jacobs insists that the risks of equity and royalty arrangements can be lessened if the deals are structured properly.

"You can't eliminate risk," Jacobs says. "But you can manage risk."

Chapter 2

Steps to Success

There are several ways to develop a mutually beneficial equity or royalty arrangement with client companies, such as monitoring companies' progress and developing action plans for providing assistance to each company. First and foremost, however, a program must develop mindful screening of potential clients. Most incubators enter into equity or royalty deals as part of the initial contract with the company. (For an exception, see details on SPEDD's program in this chapter.)

First, we'll explore the screening process for equity arrangements.

Equity Deals

How an incubator reviews a company for a potential equity deal varies from place to place. The Boulder Technology Incubator (BTI) in Longmont and Boulder, Colorado, has been taking equity in all its client companies since its inception in 1989. Jerry Donahue, executive director of BTI, credits a stringent admissions policy for the success of the program (see Appendix 1). Out of 150 applicants a year, only five make it into the incubator. BTI also has an affiliate program, and equity arrangements are struck with these clients as well.

"As soon as we get interested in a company, either as an affiliate or a resident, we start the screening process," Donahue says. First, BTI looks at the management team. "If we need to help them build a team, this will make our job longer and more difficult," says Donahue, whose concern is balancing time and expert resources against demand.

If Donahue's in-house resources are too stretched and he can't find a qualified advisor to work with the applicant, "we won't bring them in ... even if I like the company," Donahue says. If, however, BTI decides the management needs are "manageable," Donahue will agree to include refining a company's management in with its business assistance package.

Next, BTI looks at how far the product has come. "Is it still on the drawing board? Have they developed a prototype? Is the product ready for market?" Donahue asks. Once again, the applicant's progress in this area will influence Donahue's decision. If the incubator's resources are already stretched thin, taking on a "baby" company as opposed to a "toddler" may be ill advised. If all looks promising, however, "next we look at how good the actual product or service is," Donahue says. "We study the market strategy, do market research or 'sanity checks,' as we call them. We'll verify the product with outside consultants, if necessary. And the company's business plan better be decent or we'll send them back to work on it."

Most applicants who get this far have a good chance of entering into a contract with BTI. Only then do they get to what is often the first screening stage in a nonequity incubator: the incubator admissions review committee. Once this committee gives the green light of admission to the incubator, the company goes on short-term probation to make certain that both parties are compatible. "It's usually our election [to decide if they can stay]," Donahue says. "And in about 90 percent of the cases, they stick around."

Breamer of (TEA) is the "pre-review" reviewer of the extensive application package submitted by potential participants in TEA's microequity fund, which differs from a classic equity arrangement. The fund, capitalized by the U.S. Department of Energy, allows TEA to provide between $20,000 and $50,000 to small businesses in the form of a debenture note, which can later be converted to equity (see Appendix 2). The best candidates are emerging companies introducing a product for national or international sale. Potential candidates submit their application to Breamer, who works up an executive summary of the applicant's proposal for the seven-member review committee.

"If they recommend [acceptance], only then do we establish the terms of obligation," Breamer says. The deal is still not complete; the applicant must agree to those terms and win approval by TEA's full board of directors before an equity arrangement is struck. At that time, TEA sets a valuation of the company and a stock conversion ratio.

Jacobs of the Genesis Business Centers Ltd. follows a slightly different path when assessing potential deals. Genesis has taken equity in all its ten companies. As a for-profit incubator, Jacobs, who is the majority stockholder, says that "yours truly" makes the final decision on which companies are offered a contract with Genesis. When an applicant comes to him, Jacobs requires two things before he'll give the deal serious consideration: a complete business plan and a good draft of an offering memorandum. An offering memorandum, or prospectus, is a legal document put together with the help of a securities attorney that describes the company in minute detail.

"It tells you everything you could possibly want to know about the business," Jacobs explains, "including where there may be bumps in the road .... This helps one to judge whether the company's common stock is worth the offering." If a company doesn't have a prospectus, he refers it to qualified attorneys who will prepare one for a fair price.

Jacobs looks for much the same things that Donahue and Breamer look for when assessing a potential deal: management team, product viability, and product profitability. "It has to be high tech or something innovative," he says. "There must be something proprietary about the company's technology; it must be patentable for instance." And they have to have 50- to 60-percent gross margins. We want high profitability in terms of unit selling price over unit cost."

In addition, Jacobs stresses that he wants to see built into the company's future plans an exit strategy for the incubator, and he wants to make a profit from that plan. "Within three to five years — sometimes as high as seven — they have to plan on a public offering or a third-party acquisition," he says. "And they have to be selling into the market sufficiently large enough to permit the company to achieve a reasonable market share – one that translates to annual revenues of between $10 million and $50 million within five years of the time the company enters the incubator program."

Royalty Deals

The screening process for royalty arrangements follows the same general pathway and identifies similar criteria as equity arrangements. Larry Albertson, president of the North Florida Technology Innovation Corporation (NFTIC) in Gainesville, Florida, sums up his due diligence process for royalty deals succinctly: "In effect, we're taking a position on the management team, so we're looking for clients with whom we can establish that kind of relationship."

Albertson places weight on one more factor: a personal investment on the part of the entrepreneur. Quite simply, if the founder of the company isn't willing to take a risk on the business, then the incubator shouldn't be, either. NFTIC has five full-time staff and four graduate student interns who aid in performing due diligence for potential clients. Albertson says that it can take up to 90 days before a contract is signed, which is not unusual for incubators that enter into equity or royalty arrangements with clients.

Meeder makes both equity and royalty deals with select client companies. The equity arrangements allow SPEDD to have some say in how the company is run. The royalty arrangements are in place to generate earlier revenue for the incubator than equity. "It takes so long to see any sort of equity liquidated in a small company," Meeder explains, "we figure we'd be bankrupt if we tried to live on that."

Unlike the other programs mentioned here, SPEDD enters into equity and royalty arrangements with established clients or near graduates rather than new clients. These "step-up" companies, as they are called, have proven their ability to generate "business clusters," or to draw into the area a number of other companies with related market products. In addition, they have a product or service that's "'pitchable and catchable' in the community and that doesn't get bogged down in a huge capital investment," Meeder says. Out of 340 SPEDD clients, only five have been selected as step-ups. They range from a fiber optics company to an arts studio.

Developing an Action Plan

The screening process plays an important role in equity and royalty arrangements because it helps the incubator manager set up an action plan for the company.

From information gathered in the screening process, the incubator can develop a service package geared to the company's specific needs (see Case Study: Putting a Service Plan into Action, page 13). This action plan represents another crucial step in forming a fruitful equity or royalty arrangement with client companies. The services included in the plan can exceed basic incubation services. For instance, in BTI's case, the incubator makes a "best efforts" commitment to help the company land its first significant round of funding. It helps the company draft a fundable business plan, put together a package/presentation, complete due diligence, and get introductions to investors. "Everybody needs money," Donahue notes. "And if they don't have it yet, it's usually because there's a problem in one of [these] areas."

"We also massage the management team," Donahue says, because that is the area in which most companies are incomplete. "People invest in people, so [the management team] is the most important part of the equation." The team is assembled utilizing the resources of the incubator, mentors, advisors (the incubator has a network with members numbering in the three figures), and through the incubator's "dating services," as Donahue calls its capital network.

Jacobs of Genesis also focuses his resources on linking clients to potential investors. "They only get one chance to make a good first impression," he says of his clients. "If they engage in too much 'techno babble,' they're going to lose their chance. So we coach them over and over again. We then do mock presentations to prospective investors. After they gain confidence and poise in making these presentations, we put them in settings where they meet prospective investors. For instance, we'll bring tours of angels into the incubator." He adds that the group approach works to the angels' advantage, too, because the investors retain a certain amount of anonymity and feel less pressure to make a commitment than they would in a one-on-one situation.

Meeder of SPEDD creates an action plan for his equity/royalty clients. He wants these arrangements to generate revenues *and* enhance SPEDD's main mission of improving the economies of the communities it serves. "We guide the company toward economic development activities that are crucial to building a business cluster," Meeder explains. "We want to generate a whole series of companies around [the client company]."

Thus, in the action plan SPEDD takes a hands-on role in directing the company's future market products and sales. "When a company's defined as a step-up company, we take a relationship that's beyond just an incubator-tenant relationship," Meeder says. "We do hundreds of hours of work developing a marketing strategy and implementing the sales plan."

As an example, Meeder cites Prism Fiber Optics, a client who was attempting to commercialize patents in a scoping device that could allow a technician to look inside broken equipment. Though the company's device was useful, it wasn't unique in its commercial application, and its functions could be duplicated by existing technology. SPEDD recognized a better market niche for the patents — illuminated point-of-purchase signs, such as the neon signs used to advertise soft drinks. The incubator struck an equity-royalty deal with Prism, and the arrangement has proven lucrative for both parties. In the second year of the plan, Prism's sales were well ahead of schedule, with the company pulling in $3.2 million. SPEDD expects to receive $84,000 in royalty fees from Prism in 1997.

Choosing a Winner

According to incubator professionals who have entered into royalty or equity agreements with clients, the key to establishing a fruitful relationship is screening those clients carefully. Here are some tips on how to assess a potential winner.

- **Examine the company's management team.** Donahue of BTI advises bypassing a company that is weak in this area if you do not have the resources to strengthen the team. Expect, however, to spend some time with every company working to strengthen its management team. Almost every emerging company can benefit from enhancing management savvy.

- **Assess the viability of the company's product or service.** "We're looking for technology with merit," says Albertson of NFTIC. "It doesn't have to be patented, but it should have something that gives it a competitive edge."

- **Review the company's financial projections**. Equity clients should have the potential to generate high profitability in terms of gross margins and should plan to sell out in the multimillion-dollar range within five years, according to Jacobs of Genesis. For royalty clients, the guidelines are less clear, but the firms should have the ability to generate healthy sales, says Meeder of SPEDD.

- **Review the company's long-term plans.** For equity clients in particular, Jacobs cautions that an exit strategy for the incubator must be built into the company's business plan. Companies must either complete a third-party acquisition or a public offering in order for Genesis to liquidate its equity.

- **Look for a personal investment on the part of the entrepreneur.** Albertson notes that unwillingness on the part of the client to put money behind his or her own company is a definite red flag in the client's disfavor.

- **Build and retain a high-caliber cadre of experts to help assess the clients' products or services.** Incubator professionals in this book gave this tip across the board. Not one believed that he or she — or other incubator staff — had the expertise to thoroughly assess every new technology that came through the door.

Case Study: Putting a Service Plan into Action

The Boulder Technology Incubator enters into equity and, to a lesser degree, royalty deals with each of its high-tech clients. These clients come into the incubator with varying degrees of business experience. In the case we're about to explore, the entrepreneurs were true neophytes. One of the brothers was still in college, the other was drawn to Colorado for all the state has to offer. They had no business experience, no management experience. According to BTI Executive Director Jerry Donahue, however, they had a hot idea — technology used with video games — and they had already begun the first steps toward product development.

Donahue says he and his staff had little experience with video game technology. But the brothers were enthusiastic, likeable, and willing to work hard. Background checks, using their references and a list compiled by BTI, confirmed that the potential clients had solid reputations. So Donahue sought out an expert in the video game industry to assess the product while his staff began the due diligence process in-house.

"We found that the technology wasn't complete, but [our expert advisor] thought they were on to something," Donahue says. "[A] toy company had tried it before and couldn't make it work. But [the potential clients] had already made improvements on the technology."

At the same time that BTI was assessing the product, it also was taking a hard look at the clients' business plan and financial status. "They had some family money but it wasn't enough," Donahue says. "We knew we would have to immediately look for other sources of funds. Their business plan was inadequate to get those funds, so that had to be improved."

In addition, given the company's lack of experience, BTI would have to bring in a suitable management team. Again, this was an immediate need if the company were to be signed on as a client. Through BTI's network of advisors, Donahue found an experienced entrepreneur who was willing to assess the situation. Though BTI sometimes waits until the due diligence process is complete before putting together an advisory board for clients, Donahue asked the two experts on the review panel to sign on as members of the company's advisory board. Thus, the key members of the board were in place by the time the decision was made to accept the company three months later.

During the due diligence process, Donahue says there was "constant communication" between the incubator and the company. The list of services that the company would need expanded as the talks continued. Before the contract was signed, BTI presented its action plan to the company. In exchange for equity, the incubator would (1) help the company complete its business plan; (2) put together a good management team for the company and take on the role of acting management until the team was compiled; (3) put together an advisory board for the company that would change as the company's needs changed; (4) help the company complete a private placement memorandum (Used to attract investors, this is similar to, but less formal than, a letter of memorandum.); (5) locate legal and accounting expertise at a pro bono or reduced rate for help in structuring and valuing the company; (6) groom the company for presentation to angel investors; (7) locate potential sources of capital, including private investors, venture capitalists, banks, government grants, and other sources; (8) and help the company complete primary and secondary market research, including focus groups. In addition, the company was offered reduced rent, shared office services, and other standard incubator services.

BTI placed a dollar value of $300,000 on its services to the company. In return, the incubator asked for 5 percent equity. The company agreed, and the contract was signed.

Donahue says that things moved swiftly for the company from that point. One of the two initial advisory board members — the experienced entrepreneur — took a keen interest in the company. "He actually made an investment in the company and took over as chairman of the board," Donahue says. "Then he became the CEO and brought in other management talent as well."

The new CEO was also instrumental in getting the business plan together. Within sixty days of entering the incubator, the company had a plan suitable for presentation to investors. In conjunction with BTI, the CEO soon located a chief financial officer, a chief operations person, and corporate counsel for the company.

Several years later, the services offered the clients have been delivered, and the company is valued at $2 million-plus.

"They're just about to [graduate]," Donahue says. "They've had several additional rounds of funding. The one in place right now is going to raise about $6 million."

Donahue says he anticipates that the company will eventually enter a strategic partnership or go out for an initial public offering. "When you think of all the services the company got in terms of the value of the company today, [the equity deal] was a real bargain," he says.

Chapter 3

Structuring the Deal

Before entering into an equity or royalty arrangement with client companies, the business assistance program or incubator will benefit from expert advice on determining how best to structure the deal. This is especially true when it comes to drafting the contract. Also, because many incubators are nonprofits, equity and royalty revenues can impact an incubator's tax status.

"No matter how good a relationship you have starting off, you may run into some snags [with clients]," says Larry Albertson of NFTIC. A clearly written contract is the best way to avoid potential disagreements. In addition, a contract helps protect the incubator's interests. "The intent of these contracts is certainly not to drag these companies into court," Albertson stresses. "But there should be some reasonable amount of protection so that if we do our job well, we get the return we've agreed upon."

Albertson cites as an example a client who, with NFTIC's aid, has caught the interest of a major investor just six months after signing a royalty contract with NFTIC. The investor wants to take a hands-on role in directing the company's future. Given the investor's business experience, the incubator is no longer needed. Because NFTIC has a contract in place, the incubator is in a position to negotiate an advantageous way out. Albertson hopes to exchange his royalty in the company for a cash settlement and a small percentage of equity. Without the stipulations spelled out in the contract, six months of work could have been for naught. (See Appendix 6 for NFTIC's service proposals and client agreements, which work to the incubator's and clients' benefit.)

Obviously, weeks or sometimes months of ongoing communication between the incubator and client take place before a contract is signed. First, due diligence must be completed and an action plan geared to the needs of the client must be developed. Following that, the incubator must present its terms to the company for negotiation. The following section offers tips on how to arrive at a fair arrangement.

Equity and royalty deals in incubators have characteristics that depart from classic equity-royalty circumstances. For instance, when a private investor prepares to take equity in a company, he or she will rely on a complicated valuation formula to determine the rate. Valuation is the estimated dollar value placed on a company by potential investors or credit providers. However, the incubator professionals who talked with the NBIA largely veered from using a hard and fast formula to value fledgling companies. Donahue of BTI bluntly states that "valuing a start-up is a very different process from evaluating an emerging, growing business concern. They have no assets yet, no products. You can't put these elaborate quantitative measures on nothing."

The percentage of equity or royalty that the incubator receives from a company often is based on the value of the services the incubation program gives in return. Most incubators varied in how they arrived at this figure. At BTI, a potential client (no contract has been signed yet) is told what services he or she needs based on the assessment of the company completed earlier. "We base the value of the services on the real market," Donahue says. "The figure always makes the entrepreneur gulp. But then we say, 'We'll take x percent of equity in exchange for those services.' It can be as high as 10 percent but is usually around five." Most entrepreneurs jump at the opportunity. Because they probably aren't generating sales yet, "5 percent of nothing looks pretty darn good to them," he laughs. This process lets the entrepreneur know that the incubator's services have real value, and it tells them that "for better or worse, we're in this together," Donahue says.

Harlan Jacobs of Genesis tries to keep things simple for the start-ups with whom he deals. To begin, he offers to barter rent and services for the common stock or other equity security of the potential client. In most transactions, the fair market value of common stock is bartered, dollar for dollar, against the value of rent and services the company requires. (To judge the fair market value of the company's equity securities, Jacobs uses the company's business plan and its offering memorandum.) In a few select cases, Genesis will accept a flat percentage of the founder's stock, usually in the 5- to 10-percent range. This occurs when the company requests more than services or rent. "If they want me to serve on the board of directors, for instance, we'll take founder's stock," Jacobs explains.

Jacobs notes that if clients were concerned strictly with dollars and cents, they probably should have paid cash for rent and saved their stock for themselves. "But I've never had anybody come back and complain," he says. The clients got help when they needed it most, and if they paid a premium, they felt it was warranted.

Dallas Breamer of TEA takes a different approach when determining equity rates, in part due to the nature of his program. TEA has a $450,000 microequity fund capitalized by the U.S. Department of Energy. The fund allows TEA to provide a maximum of $50,000 to small businesses in the form of a debenture note, which can later be converted to equity. So TEA isn't providing services — it's providing capital in exchange for an equity option in the company.

Breamer relies on several indicators to help him set a fair equity rate, including the valuation provided by the company, the amount of money invested by the company's founders, planned future offerings, total shares of stock issued at the time the deal is struck, total investments by private sources, the value of similar market products, and his own experience at judging such deals.

Sometimes, however, the calculation is best kept simple. "If the principals have put $100,000 into the company and they own ten shares of stock, that means each share is worth $10,000," Breamer explains.

Albertson of NFTIC, who deals almost exclusively with royalty arrangements, is the first to say that his task is easier. "We lean towards royalty because with equity, you have to do a valuation ... and there's always the risk that you'll get stuck with stock that can't be liquidated," he says.

In the same spirit as Donahue, Albertson develops a joint service contract with a potential client. "The way we approach the whole issue is to sit down with the company and figure out what they need. We're looking for long-term relationships, so we do the best we can to project needs on a long-term basis — five to seven years — and also for the next twelve to twenty-four months."

Afterwards, an agreement is written up that describes the needed services. "Typically," Albertson says, "an agreement might include six to twelve tasks, like 'help to prepare initial business plan' or 'help company get access to funding.' We always write it that way — we'll help the company. We won't do it for them."

Next, timelines are assigned to the various tasks. A business plan, for instance, may take six months to complete. "We're doing this partly so that we don't overload ourselves," Albertson explains. "It allows us to prioritize."

Using the timelines as a guide, NFTIC staff members will then estimate, based on their professional experience, how many hours it will take to complete the various tasks. They then multiply estimated total hours by a blended rate of $55 per hour (blended meaning there is no distinction made between work done by professional staff or student intern). This places a dollar value on the services the incubator will provide.

"We don't assign hours per task," Albertson says. "We don't get that detailed. We just tell the client that for the first year, we are committing an average of seventy-five hours per month to you, for the second year, an average of 50 hours per month, and so on. This gives the client some feel for how much time we're investing, and, once again, it allows us not to get overloaded."

NFTIC wants a good return and is expecting to get paid for more than just time invested. "We want to get three times our investment back in five years," Albertson says. "So, if through our calculations, I come up with $100,000 worth of effort, I'm going to say I want $300,000 back. That gives me the basis for a royalty agreement. I look back at the company's sales projections — I usually don't believe them, so I adjust them until they're realistic — and set my royalty arrangement accordingly. It may take 2 percent of the company's sales to get $300,000 back within five years. It may take 5 percent. Nothing's hard and fast but it usually varies between 1 percent and 5 percent."

Meeder of SPEDD takes a common-sense approach when determining the percentage of equity or royalty he negotiates. For instance, SPEDD has a 30-percent equity option in the fiber optics company, which reflects the fact that SPEDD is more a partner than an advisor in the firm. On the royalty side, SPEDD bases its commission on the number of hours invested in the company plus the company's potential in gross sales. "We only take 2 percent royalty from the fiber optics company, but they might do a million in sales. We take a 28- to 40-percent commission from the arts studio. But the going market rate for art sales commissions is 40 percent, so they're still saving if they go with us."

Meeder adds that if the company hasn't graduated yet, they still pay for rent and services.

Other Areas to Consider

Putting a dollar value on services is a crucial part of striking a fair equity or royalty arrangement, but there are other elements that must be taken into consideration before the deal is signed. For instance, the microequity fund established by TEA does not require participants to pay on the principle of the debenture note until the note is due — usually in three years. Because of the risk involved in such deals, however, TEA attempts to recoup a 25-percent yield per year on the loan, and it does this through interest charges, fees attached to the loan, royalty fees, stock options, stock warrants, and premiums for early payments. All this is laid out before the contract is signed. Here are some other contract items to review:

• **Consider the type of equity.** BTI takes equity in the form of restricted legend stock, which means both parties usually agree when the stock is sold. In addition, the incubator's equity is "founder's stock" — the same type as the company owners have, which is issued in the beginning and for a much smaller amount per share than later stockholders pay. "When they go for additional rounds of financing, we experience dilution and appreciation the same as the founders," Donahue explains.

"We often give the first option to buy (our stock) to the principals of the company," Donahue says. The incubator put into place provisions that allow the incubator to sell its stock before the company goes public, takes on a strategic partner, or is acquired by a third party.

• **Build in flexibility.** "Negotiate terms and conditions with an eye on future investments," says Rich Bendis, president of the Kansas Technology

Enterprise Corporation (KTEC) in Topeka, Kansas. For instance, have a predetermined value that will apply if the company want to buy out its equity position early."

Albertson of NFTIC notes that a young company's situation can change drastically within a short period of time and that it's impossible to draft a contract that anticipates all contingencies. For this reason, in part, NFTIC attaches schedules to its contracts, detailing royalty payments and services rendered (See Appendix 6). "We have one company — they're doing reasonably well. But they're looking at becoming a "lifestyle" company (one that doesn't grow). They're not as interested as they orginally were in getting bigger ... so we'll have to adjust our service agreement to make it more of a maintenance agreement. Instead of providing them with a substantial amount of assistance, we're looking at just a minimum number of hours." Because the service agreement is an appendix to the contract, NFTIC will likely be able to adjust the agreement without drafting an entirely new contract.

• **Prevent misunderstanding**. "In the preclosing loan document, we express to the applicant exactly what the terms will be, so there's no misconception," Breamer says.

Albertson of NFTIC stresses that all terms and conditions should be clearly explained to the client before any documents are signed. Currently, NFTIC is in the process of revising its contract to make it more easily understood. "[The contract] is very intimidating," Albertson says. "I'd like to simplify it and shorten it." Regardless, NFTIC always advises clients to have their own attorneys study the contract.

• **Make it a two-way street.** Bendis sits in on equity negotiations between KTEC's innovation centers and the incubators' clients. He notes that the deal must be advantageous to the client as well as the incubator. He explains that private investors may shy away from a company if the incubator is perceived to have too much of a stake in the company's future.

"If you have too big of a position ... say, 50 percent equity ... it will discourage private investment, and you'll have really created an obstacle for the company," Bendis says. KTEC keeps its equity positions between 10 and 20 percent.

In addition, KTEC usually opts for common stock or convertible debt with warrants attached rather than preferred stock. Preferred stock receives "preferential treatment" over common stock. "This is a disadvantage to the company, because they don't want to establish different classes of stock. That discourages future investors," Bendis explains.

- **Set reasonable time limits.** Establish how long the deal will last, says Pruett of GENESIS. For instance, one of Pruett's clients was offered capital by a state agency in exchange for 5 percent equity over the life of the product. "We had to tell our client, 'that's a really bad deal,' and we get funded [by that agency]," Pruett laughs. "But when the company graduated, they came back to us and said that was the most valuable advice they got from us."

David Day, interim director of the University of Alabama at Birmingham's Research Foundation, handles equity and royalty arrangements with clients from UAB's incubator, the Office for the Advancement of Developing Industries. He says that the time limit for royalty deals depends largely on the product.

"If it's software, we [set the arrangement] for five to ten years because the technology changes so fast," he says. In contrast, pharmaceutical products must receive federal approval, and may take twelve years to get to the market. "We'll do that for the term of the patent, which is twenty years," Day says.

- **Review the company's corporate structure.** Incubator professionals who have entered into equity and royalty deals say the companies' sole proprietorships or partnerships must be restructured before the deal can be struck. In addition, most of the managers prefer C corporations to S corporations because the former is more attractive to potential investors. "Almost all [of the clients] are trying to raise money and sell stock, and they have to be a C corporation to do that," Albertson says. "In S corporations, all the profits and losses flow through to the shareholders. Most shareholders don't want profits showing on their personal income tax. They want capital gains, not ordinary income." Also in an S corporation, people not active in the business – those who are not partners or principals – cannot have conventional stock. Incubators take phantom stock, which essentially means they have no voting or other rights but they still gets their percentage of ownership out of the company when it is liquidated.

Companies incorporated as limited liability companies (LLCs) may pose some challenges. "It would be important to read and understand the operating agreement of the LLC to see if there are any clauses that may be inappropriate or of concern to an incubator," says Ed Sybert, director, Engineering Research Center at the University of Maryland Technology Advancement Program. "For example, the operating agreement may call for [investors] to contribute operating funds, share in expenses, or whatever. The [incubator] may or may not wish to participate in certain ways." Sybert predicts most companies that originate as LLCs will convert to C corporations within a few years to accommodate their growth. He suggests that an incubator taking equity might add a provision to an agreement with an LLC that gives the incubator an option to purchase common stock after the LLC converts to a C corporation. Or you could ask the LLC company to amend its LLC documents to render the incubator exempt from some provisions, Sybert says. Check with legal counsel on the best way to handle equity agreements with LLCs.

- **Review your program's tax status.** Theoretically, a nonprofit incubator can endanger its tax-exempt status if it has too much equity exposure in its clients, or it can run the risk of apparent conflict of interest if management stands to profit too highly from its clients' success — an example of what's known as private inurement.

If an incubator starts putting a "substantial" amount of its total assets into profit-making investments, such as equity deals, it may arouse the interest of the Internal Revenue Service. "Substantial" is a loose term, to say the least. A good rule of thumb is that equity gained should not exceed 15 percent of total assets, time invested, or any other measure of an incubator's worth. A nonprofit incubator's main purpose should be to help grow companies and create jobs — not to make profitable investments in its clients. Although the tax code does allow such investments, they should never overshadow the incubator's central task.

If the IRS discovers that a 501(c)(3) incubator is a stockholder or provider of venture capital to a client firm, the agency could deny a request for 501(c)(3) tax status, according to Janet Buehler of Coopers & Lybrand

L.L.P. Such an arrangement is called an "equity kicker." It is fine to establish some type of contract with client companies that says the incubator has a right of first refusal on the first offering of stock once the firm graduates.

Buehler notes an example of an incubator that applied for 501(c)(3) status and in every way should have qualified. It was located in a poor section of the city and could demonstrate that it helped disadvantaged individuals. In the last year of a client company's stay, though, the incubator took an equity position. The incubator's intent was to give companies an infusion of cash as they moved out on their own. The IRS saw it differently; it said everyone on the board of directors and the executive in the incubator were wealthy individuals getting a hand in the pie before companies went public.

If just giving companies cash is the issue rather than the incubator desiring a full equity-royalty arrangement, it can set up connections between the client company and a third party for the purpose of helping the new firm get an infusion of capital. This is workable as long as the third party is truly a third party and not related to someone in the incubator.

Understandably, Donahue of BTI opted for 501(c)(6) status, which does not have the private inurement rules that 501(c)(3) carries. Others, such as Dallas Breamer of TEA, have built in contingencies in case problems arise. "We're structured so that we can create a for-profit easily," Breamer says. "But so far, there's been no problem."

Others find mixed status is better all around. Bendis utilized Big Six accounting firms and several law firms when setting up the organizational structure of KTEC's innovation centers. Each center is divided into three entities. "The not-for-profit [branch] provides value-added services, training, and education," Bendis says. "Then we have a C corporation, which is our management services corporation. The president of the innovation center resides under the C corporation. He or she manages the not-for-profit entity under contract. The corporation is also the front manager of our seed capital fund, which is a limited liability company."

Approximately twenty-five clients have accessed the seed capital fund, in exchange for equity. They receive incubator services as clients of the innovation centers.

Still other incubator managers, such as Jacobs of Genesis, have elected to go with for-profit status from the start. "When we barter stock for rent, we recognize income," Jacobs says. "But it's a manageable income because ... it's offset by expenses, which means at the moment we don't have any taxable income. We will down the road when one of our companies goes public. But that's a pleasant problem to have."

An Incentive Plan for Distributing Equity

Commonly, revenues from equity or royalty arrangements are used for the incubator's operating capital. BTI, however, has developed an incentive plan wherein part of its equity is awarded to outstanding staff, advisors, and board members. "We put all stock into a combined equity pool," explains BTI Director Jerry Donahue. "Anyone who makes an extraordinary difference in the success of a company gets a small percentage of the pool as an award."

The pool is not liquid, which means awardees do not pay taxes on their equity shares until the stock has been cashed in, Donahue adds. When stock from a company is liquidated, all pool members — regardless of whether or not they worked with that particular company — receive moneys from that liquidation equal to their award percentage.

The executive committee of BTI's board of directors recommends award nominations, which are then voted on by the full board. In addition, the executive committee recommends when the equity will be liquidated. "[The awardees] do not control when they get the money — even if they leave the incubator," Donahue says.

BTI retained legal counsel when developing its shared equity plan. Donahue adds that having a securities attorney on BTI's board of directors helped make the task far easier.

Chapter 4

Drafting the Contract

While each contract is an individualized deal, there are some similarities that all share, such as the amount and type of equity or royalty granted to the incubator. The following information highlights clauses that are commonly included in equity or royalty agreements.

• **Time frames.** "Every contract needs a beginning and an end — they start on a certain day and they end on a certain day," says Donahue. In BTI's contracts, both parties generally must agree to an extension before one is granted. BTI also includes a special clause for clients who are accepted on a provisional basis — meaning that official acceptance is contingent on the results of BTI's feasibility study of the client's product. The clause basically states that the company cannot "unilaterally walk away from the deal [after it receives the results of the study] because otherwise we would be doing free feasibility studies," Donahue says.

• **Mutual obligations.** Donahue calls this the "consideration for consideration" principle. For each demand made by the incubator in the contract, the client must receive something in return. For each "demand" made by the client, the incubator must receive something in return. For the incubator, the demand may be a percentage of equity; for the client, the return demand may be an introduction to investors. Though the "consideration for consideration" principle is not a clause per se, "it is paramount to any contract," Donahue stresses.

• **Payment schedule.** Equity contracts generally include a provision detailing when payment of the incubator's equity position will occur — within a certain date following a third-party acquisition, for instance. Donahue notes that third-party acquisitions and public offerings are complicated deals, and the timing may be out of the client's hands. For that reason, he keeps this clause flexible.

Royalty payments, however, are more easily scheduled. In NFTIC's case, the payment schedule is usually added as an appendix to the contract, and may run as long as two pages (See Appendix 6). By adding the schedule as an appendix, NFTIC can easily adjust the payments should the client run into difficulties.

- **Conversion rate.** Like most entities involved in equity deals, TEA includes a standard clause stating that it can convert its debenture note into equity at a predetermined rate. However, it also has a provision allowing it to convert in steps. Breamer explains that this largely benefits the company in that the company would not have to pay back its debt in one chunk.

- **Additional payments.** This provision may cover fees for services and rent that are not covered in the equity or royalty agreement, or fees incurred in performing due diligence on behalf of the company. At times, the clause may spell out additional equity or royalty payments. BTI, for instance, will sometimes ask for "follow-up" equity if it meets a particular performance demand on the part of the client. The inclusion of this clause usually depends on the company's status. "We had one company that was pretty far along when they came to us, so we only took 2.5 percent equity up front," Donahue says. "But we included a clause stating that we'd get an additional 4 percent if we helped them get $500,000 in investments. We did, so now we have 6.5 percent of that company."

- **Penalties for late payments.** Most incubators include a clause that places a financial penalty on the client in the event of late royalty payments. At BTI, for instance, "if the royalty fee is $1,000 for April and it's now a day late, they would owe us $1,100," Donahue says. He adds that this sensitive penalty clause is negotiated with delicacy during contract discussions.

- **Service schedule.** As with its payment schedule, NFTIC attaches its schedule of business assistance services to the contract as an appendix. The service schedule, roughly two pages long depending on the client, includes benchmarks that lay out when the services will be delivered. Within six months, for instance, NFTIC might commit to helping the client complete his or her initial business plan. This approach helps clients visualize what they are getting in return for their royalties, and it helps the incubator prioritize its time and resources.

- **Authority to exercise agreement.** Many contracts include a standard clause, backed by documentation provided from the company, stating that the company is properly registered and that the owners have the authority to exercise an agreement on behalf of the company. "Basically, you want to make sure that the client is a real company," Albertson says. Details concerning the company's corporate structure also are included as a separate but related clause.

- **Insurance.** Breamer of TEA includes a clause in his contracts requiring that the key employees or owners of the company be insured. In addition, the company must have general liability insurance and product liability insurance, if applicable. Ultimately, this clause works to the benefit of both parties.

- **Employee compensation.** In order to ensure that profits from the company are used to help the company grow, TEA's contracts have a provision specifying the level of compensation for the company's employees. The terms are mutually agreed upon. "If they want to exceed [the terms], they have to get our permission," Breamer says.

- **Authority to monitor company.** Generally, an incubator will include a contract clause giving it the right to monitor the company's progress on a regular basis, including reviewing balance sheets and other financial documents. In addition to annual tax returns, TEA's clause asks the company to provide quarterly profit/loss statements, cash-flow analyses, schedules of inventory, and accounts payable. At its discretion, TEA may include a related clause requiring the company to maintain its liabilities and assets at a predetermined ratio. Breamer explains that this is done in order to forestall financial trouble.

- **Inclusion on the company's board of directors.** This clause is usually included if the incubator has a large equity or royalty percentage in the company, or if it is asked to take a leading role in the company's future development. The board seat may be voting or nonvoting, depending on how involved the incubator becomes with the client company. Jacobs of Genesis, for instance, opts for a voting seat if the company asks him to perform CEO-type duties.

- **Change of control.** Another common clause deals with a change in ownership of the company. TEA, for example, has a provision stating that if this should happen, it does not impact TEA's right to exercise its equity position in the company. A related clause states that the company cannot transfer stock without TEA's permission.

- **Arbitration.** Donahue always includes a dispute resolution clause that states that disagreements will be handled by an independent mediator. He does this in the interest of fairness and to avoid legal costs for both parties. "We haven't had to exercise it yet, but the minute I take it out, I probably will. So I'm keeping it in," he says.

    Related to this, Rich Bendis of KTEC notes that in equity deals, the client and the incubator often differ on the valuation of the company. If a predetermined formula cannot be agreed upon, he recommends including a clause in the contract stating that an independent third party will determine the value of the equity to avoid debate.

- **Default of contract.** Most contracts include a section dealing with default due to bankruptcy or other unforeseen circumstances experienced by the client. Albertson of NFTIC stresses, however, that the contract cannot cover every eventuality and that this clause, which protects the incubator, must be exercised with discretion. "If it's very early on in the relationship and the company has no assets, you may want to walk away," he says. "But if it's three years down the road and the company has $10 million in sales and then runs into problems, then there might be some company assets that you'd want to call upon."

    In addition, provisions should be included that cover unforeseen circumstances on the part of the incubator, such as shutting down operations. "Build the contract in a manner that allows you to separate on friendly terms," Bendis sums up. "If you're going to get married, you better determine how you're going to get divorced [beforehand]."

Chapter 5
Equity and Royalty in University Settings

When an incubator is an official part of a university, it usually cannot hold equity or royalty directly. But that does not stop university incubators from receiving benefits from such deals. At the University of Alabama's Office for the Advancement of Developing Industries (OADI), royalty and equity agreements are struck between the client and UAB's Research Foundation, not the incubator. "Some of the money goes to the university, some to the inventor, some to the inventor's department and part to the foundation," says Wilson Harrison, director of OADI. "Since our support comes from the university, we benefit as well."

According to David Day, interim director of UAB's Research Foundation, all intellectual property developed with university aid is assigned by contract to the foundation. "Our responsibility is to commercialize those inventions," Day explains. In most cases, the foundation will "license out" the patents to large companies that can market them effectively. Occasionally, however, the inventor — in most cases, a faculty member — wants to exploit the patent by creating a company, and the foundation will license the patent back to the inventor.

"The faculty-member company usually goes into the incubator," Day says. If [it and incubator staff] are agreeable, the foundation will negotiate an equity agreement with the start-up company, which can range from 5 percent to 20 percent, depending upon university resources utilized. (UAB receives royalty fees from every license; this ranges between 5 percent and 20 percent as well, regardless of whether the company ends up in the incubator.) "If equity is more than 5 percent, we ask for a nonvoting seat on the board of directors because we don't want our shares diluted before the company goes public," Day says. The seat gives them more input into the company's activities. Out of an average of 100 inventions a year, UAB has taken equity in ten.

The equity plan at the University of Maryland's TAP is similar to UAB's in that the university, which owns the equity, distributes cash from an equity liquidation among the incubator (which is part of the Engineering Research Center in the College of Engineering) and any other department that has been particularly helpful to that company.

TAP's equity plan has a ramp-up clause. A company must give up 1 percent equity if it remains in the incubator for a year or less. For every additional year it's there, a company gives up an additional 1 percent. "We initially had a five-year cap," says Sybert of TAP. "But that didn't work because we didn't want to kick [a client] out before they were ready. So it's been uncapped as of [1997]."

Sybert adds that the equity plan has been revised in other ways over the incubator's twelve years of existence. Originally, the university negotiated an equity deal with each client individually. Over time, however, it became apparent that companies with strong negotiating skills were striking better deals than companies with weak negotiating skills — regardless of the merits of the companies' actual products. "That was very unproductive and unfair," Sybert says.

Balancing University and Clients' Interests

Managers of university incubators may find themselves in the uncomfortable position of being an advocate for a client, while at the same time being an employee of the entity that is negotiating equity or royalty with the client. Sybert notes that a previous manager at TAP became such an strong advocate for the clients that "it definitely created a problem .... Part of the reason we fell back on [1 percent a year] equity across the board is that it takes the pressure off of everybody."

Sam Pruett, director of the GENESIS Technology Incubator at the University of Arkansas, Fayetteville, is familiar with the dilemma of balancing a client's interest against the university's interest. "The client needs to be as unencumbered as possible in order to succeed," Pruett says. "It's hard for an entity like the university to deal with small companies. The university is much more structured to deal with a large corporation, and it may not understand that these deals can make or break a small company."

In order to avoid conflict, Pruett takes on the role of diplomat when participating in negotiations that give the university the option of taking royalties down the line on a product that was developed with help from the university. "We, as an incubator, become involved by showing companies examples of how these arrangements have been done with other clients and at other universities," Pruett says.

GENESIS is aided in this task by the fact that the university's ability to stake a claim in a company is limited by a clause in the lease that reads in part:

University does not have and shall not claim any right of any nature whatsoever to inventions, patents, or other intellectual property developed by Client under this lease; provided that University may reserve rights or, at its sole option, negotiate in good faith with Client for rights to such inventions, patents, or other intellectual property if such developments are created, conceived, and/or reduced to practice through the significant or substantial assistance of University funds, faculty or staff, or University laboratories or equipment ...."

This clause, included in the GENESIS lease agreement, provides a potential source of income for the incubator, without allowing the university to interfere too much with client companies. Pruett cites the case of InvoTek, a GENESIS client that received a Phase II SBIR grant from the National Institutes of Health for the development of a laser-activated keyboard. InvoTek partnered with a university physics professor, who became the company's academic consultant and subcontractor on the project. Instead of performing the subcontract as a private consultant, the professor requested the agreement be handled through the university's Office of Research Sponsored Programs as a grant to the physics department.

"That would have put it into a whole new rule bracket," Pruett says. "The university would be going in and immediately claiming rights, not exercising the option later on, as the GENESIS lease agreement states." This requirement was not acceptable to GENESIS or its client firm.

The clause in the GENESIS lease agreement that allowed the university to claim a percentage of sales of the commercialized product and "negotiate in good faith" with the client for the patent ultimately prevailed. It allowed InvoTek to proceed with the contract without having to turn over patent rights to the university from day one. "There's no reason for you to come on the front end and tie the company's hands," Pruett told the university. "The company probably couldn't have gone into phase two funding because no [investor] would have looked at it with that many owners."

Pruett says that royalty agreements have been in place with GENESIS companies for only three years. Overall, he has mixed feelings about the advisability of entering into such deals with clients. On one hand, he notes that GENESIS could have been "rolling in money right now" had the royalty plan been around before a former client, who found a lucrative market with the auto industry, graduated. On the other hand, he sees such deals as potentially harmful to clients, who may find themselves in an awkward position when it comes to pitching their product. Pruett mentions a composting company that is attempting to sell its product to municipalities. Often, a mayor or other official will ask Pruett for his opinion on the product. "While I can't endorse any product, I can say that we've done this amount of testing and this is what we've found. But how's it going to look if I say, 'Oh, and by the way, if you buy this, I get 5 percent of the sales.'? That lowers the company's credibility."

Case Study: Clashing Over Equity

An incubator stands to reap many benefits from a relationship with a university. However, sometimes the very sponsorship that allows the incubator to flourish can be the cause of its undoing. The following case study represents a hard lesson learned by one incubator that clashed over equity holdings with its sponsoring university. For legal purposes, the names of the incubator, its director, and the university will be referred to as the Center, Director Smith, and the University, respectively.

Since its inception in the late 1980s, the Center had had a variety of local sponsors. As time passed, the University signed on as the Center's main sponsor. Though the Center was not located on university grounds, funds from the university did cover the incubator's rent. University funds did not pay the salaries of the incubator staff; however, the university did offer to run the salary payments through its own administrative office, thereby, allowing incubator staff to take advantage of the university's generous benefits plan.

"At the time, this was seen as a tremendous benefit," says Director Smith. "But it also meant that we came to be viewed, in effect, as university employees."

Like many incubators, the Center was working towards self-sufficiency. The incubator began taking equity positions in client companies to help attain this goal. "What we did — and it should have worked — was set up a for-profit entity separate from the not-for-profit incubator for the purpose of holding the incubator's equity positions," Smith explains. "We did this for legal and tax reasons, and also because it would allow the for-profit to exist separate from the university. No one knew how long the university would support the program — in fact, we anticipated that some day, we wouldn't need the university's support. The for-profit was our future."

Two years ago, the Center saw the first rumblings of financial trouble ahead when the university faced state budget cuts of its own. The university hired a senior administrator whose task was to review the budget and make cuts accordingly.

"His first question [to us] was, 'What is a business incubator?' He did not understand what we were doing but he had the authority to cut us," Smith says.

Within thirty days of taking office, the senior administrator did just that. "He flatly said, 'Come the end of this fiscal year, this program is cut,'" Smith recalls.

With six months of funding remaining, the incubator, aided by the local business community, tried hard to change the administrator's mind. "He was visited and written to by local economic development leaders, including local reps of Big Six accounting firms," Smith says. "But he was really not in tune with the university's relationship with the local business community. He was unfazed by it all."

The worst was yet to come: "Not only did he cut support, but when he realized that there were equity agreements worth six figures, his staff came to the incubator and physically confiscated the agreements.

"At the time," Smith stresses, "everyone was so focused on trying to get the university to keep funding in place, that we did not realize the full magnitude of the situation. We spent months fighting for our funding. What killed the entity in the end was that we did not understand that they were actually taking claim to the agreements."

When the reality of the situation finally sank in, the Center found itself with precious little time or resources to fight back. It could not use restricted university funds to finance a legal battle against the university. It did, however, receive some $80,000 in commitments from local business leaders to continue operations. "But without the equity, it would have been like starting from scratch," Smith says.

Thus, the decision was made, reluctantly, to close the incubator and dissolve the for-profit entity. Looking back, Smith says she would do several things differently.

First, she would structure the incubator so that no one entity could close its doors. The decision to run incubator salaries through the university, for instance, may have been ill-advised. "It was a good lesson learned in terms of sponsorship," Smith says. "You nurture a sponsor — you put their names on [your documents]. But there's a fine line between wanting them to feel a sense of ownership, and them actually feeling like they own the incubator."

In addition, Smith says she would demand an agreement with a sponsor stating that the sponsor has no claim to the equity. "I'm not sure there was anything wrong with our legal document," she says. "But I would have a more explicit written agreement with the university .... When we formed the for-profit, we made it clear [to the university] in internal documents why we were forming it. But nothing was signed formally with the university."

Lastly, Smith would not have dissolved the for-profit. "If we hadn't done that, we could have gone after the equity," Smith points out. "As it stands now, there is no entity left to go after those agreements. My own personal opinion is that the agreements are in a position where no one can cash in on them. The rightful owner no longer exists. And the university's name was never mentioned on the agreements with clients, so I don't see how they can [liquidate the shares]."

Smith adds that the incubator's demise has left a gap in the small business community. Even the University has recognized the need and is sending its SBDC [Small Business Development Center] reps on-site to local businesses. A group of community leaders are attempting to form a new incubator. Some discuss resurrecting the for-profit entity, but most are focused on the daunting task of getting a new incubator up and running.

As for the clients, Smith says that they may have to address the equity situation down the road, but thus far, it has not deterred investors from backing several former clients. "The companies may have gotten the best deal of all, because I don't think [the equity] will ever be cashed in," she says.

Summary

Whatever model you choose, here are some final points to keep in mind before proceeding with an equity or royalty arrangement:

- **Carefully review** whether these arrangements are applicable to your small business incubator.

- **Obtain competent legal** advice to review forms and agreement language.

- **Obtain the advice of a tax attorney** or accountant familiar with the specific constraints of a nonprofit while developing royalty and equity agreements.

- **Remember that these agreements are legally binding** for all signatories.

- **Thoroughly assess prospective clients** before signing a contract.

- **Ensure that royalty and equity agreements are clearly stated** and carefully explained to potential clients.

- **Keep copies of all signed agreements** and attach them to your lease documents.

The complexities of equity and royalty deals may appear daunting, but managers say that the time and effort invested are worthwhile. BTI, for instance, is starting to see some returns from its equity positions. It just realized $55,000 from a former incubator company liquidation. Along with equity that BTI realizes from incubator companies through a venture fund, BTI's portfolio of equities and royalties could see a compounded return in the mid-20 percent range. In another five years, the incubator could easily be financially independent, Donahue says.

"When I first came in January of 1993, the incubator was basically dormant and deeply in debt," he adds. "My job was to get debt off the books, get a new building, and find clients. The only thing we had to pay to creditors was our stock. It was a godsend. The incubator might not have survived if it hadn't had a pool of equity."

Appendices

These documents in these appendices are offered as models. They are printed here with the understanding that neither the author nor the publisher is engaged in rendering legal, accounting, or other professional service. For legal advice or other expert assistance, seek the services of a competent professional.

1

Colorado Venture Centers
Company Development Checklist

The following is a checklist of requirements that an emerging growth company must address during its development in order to be successful. Through our Venture Guild, our extensive network of professional service providers and in-house staff, we help our clients more efficiently address the items appropriate to their specific needs and state of development. The checklist is used to prepare a customized task plan for each client.

Business Planning

- ❑ Commercial feasibility assessment
- ❑ Commercialization strategy development
- ❑ Baseline needs assessment
- ❑ Evaluation of business plan
- ❑ Written review by experts
- ❑ MIT Forum-type review by panel of experts
- ❑ Preparation of business plan
- ❑ Classes/seminars/materials on how to write a business plan
- ❑ Assistance by experts to help write the plan
- ❑ Technology validation
- ❑ Venture structure planning
- ❑ Consultation on implementing the business plan
- ❑ Assessment of plan implementation

Market Analysis

(Primary research [surveys]; secondary research [library, database, on-line])

- ❑ Market feasibility studies
- ❑ General industry analysis
- ❑ Identification and analysis of target markets (applications)
- ❑ Customer purchase process — identify factors that influence buy decision
- ❑ Competitor analysis

Marketing Plan

- ❑ Positioning strategy development
- ❑ Distribution development
- ❑ Promotion and advertising plan
- ❑ Pricing strategy
- ❑ Sales process development

Marketing System
- Development of presentation and networking skills
- Development of presentation materials
- Assistance with identifying various reps and negotiating relationships
- Training of sales staff
- Contact management skills and systems development
- Image and branding
- Telemarketing system development
- Competitor surveillance
- Customer feedback system development
- Contract development
- Order entry, tracking systems development
- Credit processes systemization
- Accounts receivable management

Management
- Venture team building
- Recruiting board of directors/advisors
- Structuring compensation plans
- Hiring system development
- Structuring of employment agreements

Raising Capital
- Capital-raising strategies/methodologies/structuring the deal
- Identification of capital sources/introductions
- Identification of other sources of funds
- Assistance with negotiations
- Business valuation
- Legal issues/securities laws
- Prospectus writing
- Presentation materials development
- Assistance with presentations
- Planning the path to IPO
- Banking relationship maintenance
- Leasing strategies

Product
- Technology validation
- Applications definition and prioritization
- Establish alpha and beta site testing
- Prototype development referral
- Product design referral
- Product packaging referral
- New product development

Intellectual Property
- Assistance with filing
- Evaluation of IP status

- Possible infringement analysis
- Assistance to license IP
- Assistance to secure external IP

Operations
- Development of quality systems
- Preparation for ISO 9000 certification
- Preparation for ISO 14000 certification
- TQM system development
- MRP system development
- Facilities procurement assistance
- Equipment procurement assistance
- Manufacturing processes development
- Warranty and service program development

Human Resources
- System set-up, policies & manual
- Development of recruiting strategies
- Finding candidates
- Hiring and firing
- Creation of confidentiality, noncompete agreements
- Employee training development
- Structuring of compensation plan
- Performance evaluation

- Contract writing and negotiation
- Benefits package set-up
- Health care
- Retirement
- Ongoing routine assistance

Regulatory Issues
- Workshops
- Referral to regulatory experts

Accounting & Finance
- System set-up
- Ongoing routine assistance
- Raising capital issues
- Procurement of part-time CFO
- Taxes

Legal
- Start-up
- Shareholder agreements
- Ongoing routine assistance
- Securities issues for raising capital
- Confidentiality agreement

Information Management Systems
- Overall process, flow chart
- Communication processes

Administrative
- Directors and officers
- Insurance

- ❏ General liability
- ❏ Product liability
- ❏ Key man
❏ Travel
❏ Shareholder relations
❏ Shareholder, directors meetings
❏ Reports, filings

Strategic Alliances

❏ Strategies for strategic partnering
❏ Candidate identification
❏ Presentation preparation, issues and materials
❏ Contacting candidates
❏ Negotiations
❏ Types
  - ❏ Marketing, distribution
  - ❏ Manufacturing
  - ❏ R&D
  - ❏ Supplier
  - ❏ Customer

2

Convertible Debenture Note
SAMPLE

ABC CO., INC., a Washington Corporation, hereinafter called the Corporation, is indebted and, for value received, hereby promises to pay to Tri-Cities Enterprise Association $50,000.00 in legal tender of the United States of America on October 3, 2000, at the main office of Tri-Cities Enterprise Association at 2000 Logston Blvd, Richland, Washington. This Convertible Debenture Note shall be surrendered to corporation upon payment in full.

The Corporation further agrees to pay interest on the principal amount from time to time remaining unpaid thereof, from October 3, 1996, at the rate of 15% per annum, plus the additional sums hereinafter described, payable quarterly on the first day of January, April, July and October of each year.

In addition to the interest payable as described above, the Corporation shall pay to TEA .75% of the gross sales price of all Products Sold during the term of this Convertible Debenture Note. "Products Sold" shall not include consultation by the Corporation provided for a fee, which is not associated with the sale of a product sold by the Corporation.

There shall be a maximum cumulative annual yield on the obligation of the Corporation to TEA of 25% per annum in Total Return to TEA. The "Total Return" consists of the interest of 15% per annum plus the percentage paid to TEA of .75% of the gross income on Products Sold described above. In the event that the Total Return is less than 25% per annum in any year, the difference between the total amount of return paid and 25% per annum on the $50,000.00 advance shall carry over to the next year as a cumulative ceiling. The additional return to TEA of .75% of gross product sales shall be paid until the total 25% per annum for each year the note remains unpaid.

The principal hereof, the interest, and the additional sums hereon, shall be payable at the office of Tri-Cities Enterprise Association at 2000 Logston Blvd, Richland, Washington, except that, with respect to interest and the additional sums, the Corporation shall, upon request of the holder hereof, mail a check or draft representing such interest and the additional sums to the holder hereof at its address below stated.

If default be made in the payment of the principal of, interest on, or the additional sums payable under this Debenture Note, the total principal amount thereof, and all interest due thereon, including the additional sums, shall forthwith become due and payable at the option of TEA, and the corporation will immediately pay the same.

Payment to the holder hereof of principal, interest, and the additional sums shall be a complete discharge of the Corporation's liability with respect to such payment, but the Corporation may, at any time, require the presentation hereof as a condition precedent to such payment.

The holder of this Debenture Note has the right, at its option, from time to time, at any time prior to maturity, to convert all or a portion of the principal amount hereof into Common Shares of the corporation, as such shares shall be constituted at the date of conversion, at a conversion price of $5,000.00 for 1% of the outstanding stock of the Corporation, at the office of the Corporation accompanied by written notice of conversion. For purposes of this document, "Outstanding stock" shall include any stock option authorized (whether or not issued). At the time of execution of this Convertible Debenture Note there are one million shares of outstanding stock as herein above defined. Share certificates evidencing said share ownership shall be immediately issued by the Corporation. Upon such conversion, TEA shall be vested with 1% of all outstanding common stock for each $5,000.00 of principal converted, or 10% if the entire $50,000.00 obligation of the corporation is converted.

At the time of conversion, any unpaid and accrued interest on the principal balance owing shall be paid to TEA, together with additional sums accrued and unpaid pursuant hereto.

This Debenture Note may be redeemed prior to maturity, at the option of the Debtor, as a whole at any time or in part from time to time, at the office of Tri-Cities Enterprise Association, upon the notice referred to below, at the following redemption prices (expressed in percentages of principal amount) together with accrued interest and additional sums accrued to the date fixed for redemption. Notwithstanding any other provision herein to the contrary, in the event of redemption prior to maturity, all unpaid earned interest and royalties shall be paid to the date of redemption, in addition to the redemption payoff amount specified below.

Time of Redemption	Percentage of Principal Amount
If redeemed within 1 year of issue	110%
If redeemed within 2 years, but after 1 year	108%

If redeemed within 3 years, but
after 2 years   105%
If redeemed any time after 3 years   103%

Notice of redemption to the holder of the Debenture Note shall be given to Tri-Cities Enterprise Association at its office at 2000 Logston Blvd, Richland, Washington 99352, with the payment by cashier's check in the sum hereinabove provided with interest to the date of payment.

IN WITNESS WHEREOF, the Corporation has signed and sealed this Debenture Note on October 3,1996.

ABC CO., INC.
BY: _____
BY: _____

STATE OF WASHINGTON)
                                    : SS.
COUNTY OF BENTON   )

I certify that I know or have satisfactory evidence that_____ and _____ signed this instrument, on oath stated that they were authorized to executed the instrument as the _____ and _____, respectively, of ABC CO., INC., and acknowledged it to be the free and voluntary act of such corporation for the uses and purposed mentioned in the instrument.

GIVEN under my hand and official seal this 3rd day of October, 1996.

Notary Public in and for the State of Washington, residing at

_____

3

**Tri-Cities Enterprise Association
SAMPLE: Agreement Relating to
Convertible Debenture Note**

THIS AGREEMENT is made this 3rd day of October, 1996, by and between TRI-CITIES ENTERPRISE ASSOCIATION, whose address is 2000 Logston Blvd, Richland, Washington 99352, hereinafter referred to as "TEA", and ABC CO., INC., a Washington corporation, hereinafter collectively referred to as "Debtor" or "the Corporation".

Debtor is borrowing funds from TEA, which will be repaid by Debtor, or converted to common stock at the option of TEA. The terms and conditions relating to the aforementioned loan are set forth in this Agreement Relating to Convertible Debenture Note and other associated documents. NOW, THEREFORE, in consideration of the mutual promises and covenants herein contained, the parties agree as follows:

1. Loan: TEA hereby agrees to loan, and Debtor hereby agrees to borrow the sum of $50,000.00 to be disbursed upon execution of this agreement and the documents hereinafter identified, and upon receipt of the funds from the United States Department of Energy. This Agreement is contingent upon receipt of funds from the United States Department of Energy by TEA in sufficient amount to provide the $50,000.00 loan herein described. Loan and interest thereon shall be paid to TEA by the Debtor according to the terms of the attached Convertible Debenture Note, marked Exhibit A, which is hereby incorporated herein

2. Additional Documents: Each of the parties hereto agree to execute and deliver to one another such further documents as may be reasonably requested for any one or more of the parties hereto as are determined necessary to fully effectuate all of the terms, provisions and understandings of this agreement.

3. Assignment: The terms and provisions of this agreement are personal to the Debtor and Debtor may not assign, transfer or sell its rights under this agreement without the express written consent of TEA obtained in advance. 4.

4. Insurance Coverage: The Debtor shall be required to maintain life insurance, at its expense, payable to TEA through escrow, which life insurance shall be in an amount sufficient at all times to pay the obligation due TEA hereunder in full. Said life insurance shall be carried on the life of KEY EMPLOYEE, and shall have a face value sufficient to pay all the obligations due to TEA hereunder in full. Copies of all such life insurance policies shall be delivered to

TEA, along with the assignments of beneficial interest in said policy in the form attached hereto, naming TEA as beneficiary, and the Debtor may not change the beneficiary upon said policy until such time as the obligations hereunder are paid in full, or, until the Debtor has obtained the written consent of TEA in advance. Further, the Debtor shall require the insurance company to provide TEA with a ten (10) day notice by registered mail of any cancellation or change affecting the interest of TEA.

5. Insurance: The Debtor shall carry and maintain full and general liability insurance, including, if demanded by TEA, products liability insurance, in an amount of not less than $1,000,000.00 coverage. PROVIDED, TEA shall not have the right to demand products liability insurance until Debtor begins the manufacture of a product for sale.

The Debtor shall deliver copies of the policies and receipts showing payment of the premiums to the insurance company to TEA at convenient intervals, but not less often than annually.

Additionally, all such insurance shall be written with responsible companies, and all policies shall require notice by registered mail to TEA of any cancellation or change affecting any interest of TEA and TEA's security, which notice shall be given at the same time and contemporaneous with the notice given to the Debtor.

6. Covenants by Debtor:

During the term of this agreement, the Debtor covenants and agrees to perform the following:

(a) During the term of this agreement, unless waived in writing by TEA, the Debtor shall be required to conduct its affairs in a financially responsible manner. Debtor shall employ generally accepted accounting principles in maintaining its financial books and records, and TEA shall have the right to audit Debtor's records upon reasonable notice, at TEA's

discretion, and expense.

(b) The Debtor agrees that it shall not pay, transfer or convey to its stock owners any proceeds from the Debtor by any means, including, but not limited to, compensation, dividends, bonuses, loans, pension or profit sharing plan payments, value of fringe benefits, savings plans, or any other form of compensation or proceeds in excess of $5,000.00 total per month to key employee or the owner during any fiscal year of the Debtor without the prior written consent of TEA.

(c) The Debtor agrees that TEA's conversion rights as described in the Convertible Debenture Note shall remain at 1% of the outstanding stock for each

$5,000.00 of principal on the loan, regardless of future stock issues; that is, TEA's equity position in Debtor upon conversion shall not be diluted lower than 1% of the outstanding stock for each $5,000.00 of principal without TEA's prior written agreement. d) All currently owned and any new or additional technology developed or acquired by Debtor, and any patent or license rights associated therewith, shall be retained by the Corporation until all obligations to TEA described herein are completed, and as long as TEA is shareholder, whichever occurs last. It is the intent of the parties hereto that as long as TEA is either a debenture note holder or an equity interest owner, that there will be no transfer by ABC Co., Inc. or its principals of any technology that was developed or owned by the Debtor.

7. Default, Pledge, Sale, and Execution on Security: In the event of any default under the terms and provisions of this agreement (including the default under any of the provisions of any attachments hereto incorporated into this agreement), TEA shall notify Debtor of such default, in writing:

(a) If the default is a default in the payment of the amounts due Seller hereunder, said default shall be remedied within 10 days of said notice, and, in the event the payment is not remedied within said 10 day period, then, at the election of TEA, the entire remaining unpaid balance due to TEA shall be due and payable at once, and TEA shall be authorized to exercise any and all remedies provided it under the terms and provisions of this agreement and at law and equity.

(b) If the default is a default other than a payment of sums due to TEA, then, in that event, TEA shall give Debtor written notice of said default, and the Debtor shall have a 30 day period in which to cure said default; provided, however, TEA reserves the right to take all steps necessary as determined by TEA to reasonably protect TEA'S interest, and to mitigate TEA's damages, including, but not limited to, making payments on or behalf of the Debtor. Debtor shall immediately repay all sums to TEA upon demand.

(c) Any default in any of the terms or provisions of this agreement shall, subject to the notice periods above, and the rights granted herein, be treated as a default in the Convertible Debenture Note (the "Note"), and the rights granted to TEA in the event of default in the payment of the Note, or any installment thereof, shall be available in the event of such default of any covenant, promise, term or condition of this agreement, or any

attachment hereto.

(d) In the event of any default and after expiration of any time to cure as described in paragraphs 8(a) and 8(b) by the Debtor, TEA shall have the right to accelerate payment of the entire balance due to TEA.

(e) Time is of the essence hereof, and, if the Debtor defaults in the performance of this agreement, or any of the terms and conditions of this agreement, and said default is not cured within the time periods set forth herein above, TEA may pursue any and all rights and remedies provided in this agreement, the Convertible Debenture Note, as well as all rights and remedies available to the TEA at law and equity, or any combination thereof. Any and all such rights and remedies shall be accumulative to the maximum extent of law and equity. Further, in the event of any inconsistency with respect to any such rights and/or remedies, TEA may elect with respect thereto at any time.

8. Notices: Any notices to be given under the terms of this agreement shall be sent by certified mail, return receipt requested, to Debtor, as necessary, setting forth the nature of the default. On or after the last day of the respective notice period as provided above, TEA shall have the right to exercise any and all remedies as afforded by this agreement. A notice, communications, or demand to be given hereunder shall be given in writing and sent by certified mail, return receipt requested, as provided herein, addressed as follows:

DEBTOR:
ABC Co., Inc.
1000 Lee St.
Kennewick, WA 99336

TEA:
2000 Logston Blvd
Richland, Washington 99352

The foregoing addresses may be changed by either of the parties giving written notice to the other party of such change.

9. Representations and Warranties:

(a) Debtor represents and warrants that:

(i) Debtor has one million shares of stock outstanding which is owned by_____, _____, &_____. Said stock is free and clear of all encumbrances;

(ii) Debtor has full authority to enter into this transaction, including the right to issue the Convertible Debenture Note relating thereto.

> (iii) This agreement, and all of its terms and conditions, are fully binding upon Debtor.

10. Indemnity: Each party agrees to indemnify the other against, hold theother harmless from any liability, cost, expense, or damage, including, without limitation, reasonable attorney's fees, disbursements and court costs occurring or resulting from the incorrectness of any representations and, warranties made by any one party to another in this agreement or any breaches by any one party or default by any one party under the covenants, representations, warranties, or other provisions of this agreement.

Further, any default by any one party with respect to this agreement or any of the terms or provisions hereof, which results in any sum being due by one party to the other, such sums shall bear interest at the rate of 25% per annum from the date incurred until paid. Additionally, any default in any installment due to TEA or the balance due to TEA in the event of an acceleration of the entire loan balance shall, from the date of default, bear interest at the rate of 25% per annum until paid.

Further, any collection costs, court costs, attorney's fees incurred by any one party in enforcing this agreement, or by TEA enforcing any of the defaults of the Debtor under the obligations due TEA, shall be reimbursed to the prevailing party by the party liable to perform the same, and shall bear interest from the due date until paid at the rates and as provided for under the terms of this paragraph.

11. Merger, Negotiations, Waiver and Modification: This agreement may not be amended, modified, superseded or canceled, and none of the terms, covenants, representations, warranties or conditions may be waived, except by written instrument executed by TEA and the Debtor. All prior negotiations and understandings between the parties are merged into this agreement. The failure of any party at any time or times to require strict performance of any provision hereof shall not in any manner effect the right of such party at a later time to enforce the same. No waiver of any nature, whether by conduct, course of dealing or otherwise, in any one or more instances, shall be deemed to be or construed as a further or continuing waiver of any such condition or breach, or as a waiver of any other condition or any other breach of any other term, covenant, representation or warranty of this agreement.

12. Waiver of Security Law: The parties recognize and agree that this transaction may be covered by federal and state security laws, rules and regulations, and each party waives the application of all such rules and regulations with regard to this loan if converted to stock.

13. Attorneys Fees: Except as otherwise specifically provided for in this agreement or any attachments hereto, in the event of any dispute arising out of this agreement, the prevailing party in any such dispute shall be entitled to recover its costs, together with reasonable costs of litigation, including reasonable attorney's fees and costs of any appeal thereof.

14. Successors in Interest: This agreement shall be binding upon the parties, their successors and assigns.

15. Drafting: It is acknowledged that this agreement has been drafted by TEA's attorneys, McKinlay, Hultgrenn & VanderSchoor, and that the terms and provisions hereof have been fully negotiated, with each party having the opportunity and right, prior to execution hereof, to seek their own independent counsel. Therefore, the terms and provisions of this agreement shall not be interpreted against TEA as a result of the drafting hereof by TEA's attorneys. Debtor has had the opportunity to consult its own attorneys with regard to any questions it has about this transaction or the transaction documents. Debtor further understands that no representation has been made by TEA or TEA's agents regarding tax implications of this transaction, and Debtor has been advised to obtain advice of its own counsel and tax advisors.

16. Execution in Counterpart: This agreement may be executed in counterpart, with the total of all counterparts comprising the entire agreement. 17. Survival of Representations and Warranties: The warranties, representations and agreements set forth herein shall continue in full force and effect and shall survive the closing hereunder.

18. Loan Fee: ABC Co., Inc. shall pay to TEA at closing a non-refundable loan fee of $1,000.00.

19. Supplying of Records: Debtor agrees that it will cause to be provided to TEA quarterly in-house financial statements of the Corporation, annual non-audited financial statements of the Corporation prepared by a CPA, and a copy of the Corporation's annual income tax return. Said financial statements of the Corporation shall include, but not be limited to, a profit and loss statement, a balance sheet, and a schedule of aged accounts receivables, a schedule of inventory, a schedule of accounts payable, and a cash flow analysis. Debtor further agrees to provide such other reasonable documents and accountings concerning the Corporation as may be reasonably requested by TEA to enable TEA (to TEA's reasonable satisfaction) to determine Debtor's compliance with the provisions hereof. Further, upon request, TEA shall be authorized to review all corporate documents, minutes and records of the Corporation, and shall be authorized entry upon the Corporation's premises for such reviews, either personally or through agents of TEA, upon reasonable notice given to Debtor

IN WITNESS WHEREOF, the parties have executed this Agreement on the day and year first above written.

TRI-CITIES ENTERPRISE ASSOCIATION

By: _____

DEBTOR:

ABC CO.

By: _____

By: _____

STATE OF WASHINGTON)

: SS.

COUNTY OF BENTON)

I certify that I know or have satisfactory evidence that Dallas E. Breamer signed this instrument, on oath stated that he/she is authorized to executed the instrument as the President of TRI-CITIES ENTERPRISE ASSOCIATION, and acknowledged it to be the free and voluntary act of such corporation for the uses and purposed mentioned in the instrument.

DATED this 3rd day of October, 1996.

Notary Public in and for the State of Washington residing at

_____

STATE OF WASHINGTON)

                                    : SS.

COUNTY OF BENTON   )

I certify that I know or have satisfactory evidence

that_____and _____

signed this instrument, on oath stated that they were authorized to executed the instrument as the _____ and

_____, respectively, of ABC CO., INC., and acknowledged it to be the free and voluntary act of such corporation for the uses and purposed mentioned in the instrument.

GIVEN under my hand and official seal this 3rd day of October, 1996.

                                                     Notary Public in and for the
                                                     State of Washington, residing at

                                                     _____

4

Tri-Cities Enterprise Corporation
Microequity Fund Appliation Document Check List

1. Completed application and nonrefundable $100 application fee
2. Copy of business plan, including any description of business relationships (support from others, coventures, etc.) and resumes of principals
3. Copies of pertinent patents, if applicable
4. Authorization to conduct credit check from all principal stockholders and company
5. Personal financial statements
6. Business financial information:
    a. Income statement (profit and loss)
    b. Balance sheet
    c. Cash flow projections: monthly for first year and quarterly for years two and three
7. Recent corporate tax return
8. Articles of incorporation
9. By-laws
10. Washington certificate of incorporation from Secretary of State
11. Corporate minutes to support election of corporate officers
12. Authorization to obligate company (from by-laws or minutes)
13. Listing of stock issued, number of shares and who issued to
14. Total number of shares authorized

5

ACE-Net Terms for Angel Financing

Rich Bendis of Kansas Technology Enterprise Corporation does not have a standard document he uses when drafting equity agreements because, like other incubator professionals, he recognizes that every company is quite different. He does use as a very basic reference the ACE-Net Terms for Angel Financing. ACE-Net is the Angel Capital Network, a nationwide Internet-based listing service that provides information to angel investors on small, dynamic, growing businesses seeking $250,000 to $5 million in equity financing. It is sponsored by the Office of Advocacy of the U.S. Small Business Administration.

ACE-Net

Terms for "Angel" Financing

> **Legal Disclaimer**
>
> *This document is offered merely as a model for certain private placement stock purchase agreements. Its applicability may be limited by state law and the circumstances associated with a particular transaction. It is offered with the understanding that neither the author nor the publisher is engaged in rendering legal, accounting, or other professional service. For legal advice or other expert assistance, the services of a competent professional should be sought.*

ASSUMPTIONS

These are the assumptions under which the following Stock Purchase Agreement may be used for "angel" financing. If the facts differ from the assumptions, then the Stock Purchase Agreement may have to be modified, or the facts changed to fit the assumptions.

- The Company can issue only Common Stock.
- The Company, at the time of the "Angel" financing, is not a public company.
- The Common Stock has only one vote per share, there is no cumulative voting, and the charter and by-laws of the company have no provisions affecting voting rights.
- The Common Stock has no pre-emptive rights (meaning that every time additional stock is issued, the holder of the common stock does not have the right to purchase more stock to maintain its percentage interest in the company). (*Note:* Certain state laws provide for such pre-emptive rights unless nullified in the company's charter documents.)
- The Common Stock sold under this Agreement is newly issued stock, bought from the company (not the entrepreneur) for cash, certified check, or wire transfer.
- If the Company has any debt, it cannot be converted into stock and lender cannot exercise any control unless the Company defaults.
- The Company is a "C" Corporation under the Internal Revenue Code, meaning that the Company itself pays income taxes.
- The Investor (which would include a group of investors who are investing together and are willing to exercise rights through one representative) is accredited as is each member of any group of investors.
- The Investor is willing to provide active guidance to the entrepreneur, and the entrepreneur is willing to listen to the investor.
- All of the existing stockholders of the company, the company itself, and each of the investors will sign this agreement.

The date of this document is _____, 199_. These assumptions and the Stock Purchase Agreement that follows should be reviewed (and, if necessary, revised) no later than five years from this date so that it sufficiently reflects market conditions for this type of investment.

STOCK PURCHASE AGREEMENT

Among

_____ (*Company*),

_____ (*Investor*) and

_____ (*Stockholders*)

_____ (*Date*)

I. OWNERSHIP

(Who is investing how much for what percent of the company)

Purchase, Sale, Payment.

The Investor(s) identified on Exhibit A to this Agreement (referred to as "Investor" in this Agreement) is hereby buying _____ shares of common stock which equals _____ percent of the outstanding shares of the company (including the shares being bought by Investor) at a price of _____ per share for a total investment of _____ [*insert price per share times number of shares being bought*]. This agreement will be signed, the Investor will receive the shares and full payment (by cash, certified check, or wire transfer) will be made simultaneously. If there are any options outstanding, the parties will have determined whether or how they affect the calculation of investor's percentage.

II. CONTROL, GOVERNANCE, AND ADMINISTRATION

(Who has a say in which decisions.)

This section contains various rights of the Investor if the Investor has and maintains a certain level of investment in the company. If the Investor has this level of investment, and wants to exercise some or all of the rights listed below, the Investor may do so by placing a check mark or "x" in the space beside the right, although for the first right relating to the number of directors, all parties must also agree on the numbers of directors and insert those numbers in the blanks. Placing the check mark or "x" (and filling in blanks where necessary) will automatically adopt the paragraphs that are referenced. Parties may (but do not have to) cross out the paragraphs describing rights which are not being exercised. All parties to this agreement agree to take all steps necessary to implement the provisions selected below.

If an Investor invests so that

   (a) the amount of cash the Investor has paid for the shares bought equals 50% or more of total book value of the Company, or

   (b) the Investor owns at least 30% or more of the voting stock of the Company, and

   (c) as long as the Investor has this position,

then the Investor, if it places a check mark or an "x" in the space beside the right (and any blanks in the right are filled in), shall have:

1. _____. The right to appoint and/or nominate _____ director(s) of the total number of _____ directors of the Company. The parties agree to vote for each other's nominees for director and will provide irrevocable proxies as necessary;

2. _____. The right to approve any change to the salary of the highest paid three individuals in the Company, at least one of which will have approval on any salary taken by the Investor;

3. _____. The right to buy any securities sold by the company (except for stock options issued to employees totaling not more than ten percent (10%) of the outstanding stock of the Company) to maintain the investor's percentage interest in the Company;

4. Any or all of the following rights, irrespective of whether the Investor takes a board seat, if checked or marked with an "x":

(a) _____. to countersign all checks or other means of payment in excess of ten percent (10%) of the amount invested by Investor (*Note:* this may require redoing the company's bank resolutions);

(b) _____. to appoint the Chief Financial Officer;

(c) to approve:

(i) _____. sale of the Company or substantially all of its assets;

(ii) _____. amendment of certificate of incorporation and by-laws;

(iii) _____. the annual business plan and budget of the Company;

(iv) _____. establishing or acquiring any subsidiary or ownership interest in any entity;

(v) _____. contracts or other commitments in excess of the amount invested by the Investor;

(vi) _____. changing the legal form of the Company (such as from a "C" Corporation to a Limited Liability Company, for example, the principal office or the name of the Company;

(vii) _____. dissolving the Company;

(viii) _____. mortgaging assets of the Company and/or subjecting the assets of the Company to liens;

(ix) _____. selling Company assets other than in the ordinary course of business;

(x) _____. borrowing money for any one transaction (or series of related transactions) in amounts in excess of the amount invested by Investor unless provided for in a business plan approved by the Investor;

(xi) _____. guaranteeing the obligations of others;

(xii) _____. selecting auditors for the Company;

(xiii) _____. granting licenses of the Company's core technology;

(xiv) _____. approving, modifying, or terminating a contract between the Company and an officer, stockholder, or affiliate of the Company;

(xv) _____. employing an individual who is a relation of an officer, stockholder, or affiliate of the Company;

(xvi) _____. changing the size of the board of directors of the company;

(xvii) _____. declaring dividends;

(xviii) _____. creation of any committee of the board of directors.

5. ALL OF THE RIGHTS IN THIS SECTION II TERMINATE UPON A SUBSEQUENT PUBLIC OFFERING OF THE COMPANY'S STOCK PURSUANT TO SECTION 5 OF THE SECURITIES ACT OF 1933 OR REGULATION A OR RULE 504 OF REGULATION D, OR ANY OTHER LAW, RULE, OR REGULATION REPLACING OR SIMILAR IN FORM AND NATURE TO THEM.

III. NEXT STAGE

(*What happens to the investor when the company needs more money, goes public, or the original stockholders or the investor want to sell their shares*).

1. **Rights to Buy a Selling Stockholder's Shares.** If a stockholder (including the Investor) wishes to sell any or all of his or her shares, the company has the first right (a "right of first refusal") to buy them. If the company does not want to buy them, another stockholder or stockholders, (including the Investor), can buy them. If neither the Company nor the other stockholders (including the Investor) wants to buy them, the shares can be sold to a third party (who must agree to be bound by this Agreement as part of the purchase and may not vary any of the elections made under paragraph 4 above). The procedures to be followed are described in Exhibit B attached to this Agreement. The transfer will be subject to compliance with any applicable (at that time) federal or state laws or regulations.

2. **"Tag Along" Rights (Rights to Sell Shares When Other Stockholders Sell Shares).** If the other stockholders do not exercise their rights of first refusal and the selling stockholder (or group of stockholders acting together, which can include Investor) wishes to sell more than ten percent (10%) of its shares to another party (the "Purchaser") who is not a stockholder, then if that selling stockholder controls fifty percent (50 %) or more of the outstanding common stock, the other stockholders (including the Investor) may (but do not have to) require the Purchaser to buy the same percentage of their shares as the percentage sold by the selling stockholder (or stockholders as a group). The procedures to be followed are described in Exhibit C attached to this Agreement.

3. THESE RIGHTS TO BUY AND "TAG ALONG" RIGHTS DESCRIBED IN PARAGRAPHS 1 AND 2 ABOVE TERMINATE UPON A PUBLIC OFFERING OF THE COMPANY'S STOCK.

4. **Rights When the Company Goes Public.** When the Company goes public, that is when the Company registers its securities in a public offering, except where it is registering only securities for employee plans like a stock option plan, the Investor can "piggyback" the registration of its shares onto that registration, meaning that the Investor can have its own shares registered so they can be traded in the open market. The expense of this "piggyback" registration largely will be paid for by the Company. This "piggyback" registration right is subject to the right of the Company and its underwriters in any public offering to reduce the number of shares proposed to be registered in view of market conditions (to avoid adversely affecting the Company's offering) and any state laws or regulations which may prevent sale of these shares. Investor will retain its "piggyback" registration rights to the extent needed to sell its stock in the future. The procedures to be followed are described in Exhibit D attached to this Agreement.

IV. MISCELLANEOUS

1. **Representations and Warranties.** The Company and the Investor are making certain representations and warranties related to the condition of the company, the shares, authorization of the transaction, the sophistication of the investor, access to information and, if applicable, the authorization of the transaction, and the stock being purchased. These representations and warranties are found in Exhibit E attached to this Agreement. By signing this Agreement, the parties make these representations and warranties to each other.

. Legal Opinions. Counsel to the Company and, in certain circumstances, the Investor will provide to the other as a requirement for completion of this transaction the opinions found in Exhibit F attached to this Agreement.

. Legends to Be Placed on Stock Certificates. The certificate(s) representing the shares being purchased by the Investor shall have written on them ("legends") notification of the transfer and restrictions described by this Agreement as set forth in Exhibit G attached to this Agreement.

. Confidentiality. All information provided by the Company to the Investor or the Investor to the Company in connection with this Agreement and about the Company and its operations shall be kept confidential unless otherwise agreed to in writing.

. Other Provisions. These are additional terms to which the parties are agreeing. Although they are listed under the heading "Other Provisions," they are still important. Some of the more important ones are listed below; the others are in Exhibit H to this Agreement.

(A) All parties to this agreement agree to take all steps necessary to implement the provisions of this agreement.

(B) The terms and conditions of this Agreement shall inure to the benefit of and be binding upon the respective successors and permitted assigns of the parties. (This means, for example, if someone sells his or her stock to someone who is not a stockholder or Investor, that person will be bound by this Agreement and have the rights, restrictions, and obligations as if they were a stockholder or Investor.)

(C) This Agreement may be executed in two or more counterparts (identical copies), each of which shall be an original, but all of which together shall constitute one and the same instrument (Agreement).

(D) A written document signed by the parties is necessary to amend this Agreement or to waive the observance of any term of this Agreement (either generally or in a particular instance and either retroactively or prospectively).

(E) The Exhibits to this Agreement shall be considered part of and incorporated in this Agreement. (This means that, while certain terms have been placed in Exhibits for convenience, they are still as binding as if they were contained in the Agreement itself. Please read them carefully with that in mind; they are part of what you are agreeing to.)

IN WITNESS WHEREOF, the parties have executed this Agreement as of the date first written above.

_____ [insert name of company]

By:_____ [insert name of authorized officer]
Name:
Title:

INVESTOR(S)

STOCKHOLDER(S)

_____   _____

_____   _____

_____   _____

EXHIBIT "A"

Investor(s)

Name(s) and Social Security or Taxpayer ID No(s)	Addresses	Number of Shares Purchased

EXHIBIT "B"

Procedures to be used when a stockholder is selling its shares (right of first refusal).

Prior to making any sale or transfer of Company shares pursuant to Section III. 1, whoever wishes to sell shares (the Selling Stockholder(s)), shall give the Company the opportunity to purchase those shares in the following manner.

(a) the Selling Stockholder(s) shall give notice (the "Transfer Notice") to the Company and to each of the other stockholders (including the Investor) in writing of such intention specifying the amount of shares proposed to be sold or transferred, the proposed price per share (the "Transfer Consideration"), and the other material terms upon which such disposition is proposed to be made.

(b) The Company shall have the right, exercisable by written notice given by the Company to the seller within thirty calendar days after receipt of the Transfer Notice, to purchase all or part of the shares specified in such Transfer Notice on the terms set forth in the Transfer Notice; provided, however, if the Transfer Consideration is other than cash, the Company may pay such amount in cash equal to the fair market value of such Transfer Consideration.

(c) If the Company does not exercise its right of first refusal at all or determines not to purchase all the shares within thirty calendar days after receipt of the Transfer Notice, the other stockholders (including the Investor) shall have the right to purchase the shares the Company is not buying, exercisable by written notice given by such stockholders to the seller within forty-five days after the Company's receipt of the Transfer Notice. If more than one other stockholder gives written notice of intention to exercise this right of first refusal, the electing stockholders shall be entitled to purchase the seller's shares in amounts agreed among themselves or, if they cannot agree, in proportion to their percentages of ownership of the total number of shares held by stockholders who are purchasing.

(d) If the Company or other stockholder(s) exercises this right of first refusal, the actual purchase of the securities will take place within ninety days after the Company, or such stockholder(s), gives notice of such exercise (or such longer period set forth in the Transfer Notice), which period of time shall be extended, as necessary, in order to comply with applicable securities and other applicable laws and regulations. Upon exercise of this right of first refusal, the Company or other stockholder(s) and the seller shall be legally obligated to consummate the purchase contemplated and shall use their best efforts to secure any required approvals.

(e) If neither the Company nor other stockholder(s) exercises a right of first refusal hereunder (or all shares being sold are not purchased) within the time specified for such exercise, the seller shall be free, during the period of one hundred twenty (120) calendar days following the expiration of such time for exercise, to sell the securities not purchased at a price not less than the

Transfer Consideration and on terms not more favorable to the seller. The purchaser must agree to be bound by the terms of this Agreement as part of the purchase.

EXHIBIT "C"
"Tag Along" Rights

(a) Any stockholder (or group of stockholders acting together, which can include Investor) (the "Selling Stockholder(s)") who wishes to sell the shares it owns or controls must first give the other stockholders the opportunity to buy them following the procedures set out in Exhibit B. If the other stockholders do not wish to buy those shares, they can be sold to another party (the "Purchaser"), who must agree to the terms of this Agreement, unless the Selling Stockholder(s) controls fifty percent (50%) or more of the outstanding common stock of the Company. If that is the case, then the Selling Stockholder(s) may sell up to ten percent (10%) of the Company's stock it owns during any 365-day period without the Purchaser agreeing to the terms of this Agreement.

(b) If Selling Stockholder(s) wishes to sell more than (10%) of the Company's stock it owns during any 365-day period then it must as a condition of the sale require that the Purchaser buy the same percentage of the shares of the Company's stock held by other stockholders as the percentage of the stock being sold by the Selling Stockholder(s).

(c) The Purchaser will send written notice of its intention to purchase the Company's stock from the Selling Stockholder(s) to the other stockholders stating the number of shares it intends to purchase, the percentage of the total Company shares owned by the Selling Stockholder(s) that it is purchasing, the price, and other terms of the purchase and reminding the other stockholders that they may also sell up to the same percentage of their shares to the Purchaser in accordance with these procedures. The other stockholders will each have fifteen (15) calendar days from the receipt of this notice (the "Fifteen-Day Period") to inform the Purchaser in writing whether or not it will sell shares to Purchaser and, if so, how many. Failure to respond will mean that the stockholder does not want to sell any shares.

(d) If a stockholder wants to sell shares, then the Purchaser, if it so desires, will either purchase more shares then originally anticipated, or, if it does not wish to do so, will decrease the number of shares purchased from the Selling Stockholder(s) to accommodate purchases from the other stockholders. However, in no event will the Purchaser ever purchase in this transaction a greater percentage of the Company shares owned or controlled by each of the other stockholders than the percentage of the Company shares owned or controlled by the Selling Stockholder(s).

(e) The closing of this purchase will take place no later than thirty (30) calendar days from the end of the Fifteen-Day Period.

EXHIBIT "D"
"Piggyback" Rights

(a) If the Company intends to file a registration statement (other than pursuant to a Form S-4, S-8, or Form S-1 solely covering an employee benefit plan) in connection with the proposed sale of any of its securities either for its own account or the account of any other security holder, the Company will give written notice of its intent to the Investor. The Investor may, by delivery of written notice to the Company to be delivered no later than twenty (20) days after its receipt of the Company's notice, require that the Company include all or any part of Investor's Common Stock in such registration statement. The Company will use diligent efforts in good faith to cause such registration statement to become effective.

(b) If the proposed registration of securities by the Company is for a public offering involving an underwriting, the Investor's rights under this Section shall be conditioned upon the Investor (together with the Company and other securities holders participating in the offering) entering into an underwriting agreement in customary form with the underwriter(s) and undertaking customary related obligations.

(c) Notwithstanding any other provision of this Section, if the managing underwriter of an offering advises the Company and Investor that in its good faith judgment, the total number of shares to be registered under this Section, together with all other shares to be included in the offering, exceeds the maximum number of shares which can be sold at a price acceptable to the Company, then the number of shares of the Investor and other persons having registration rights to be included in the offering shall be reduced to that number of shares which in the good faith judgment of the managing underwriter can be sold in such offering (except for the shares to be issued by the Company, which shall have a priority). All securities of the Investor which are excluded from the underwriting for any reason shall be withheld from the market by the Investor for a period determined by the managing underwriter to be necessary to effect the offering, not to exceed 120 days.

EXHIBIT "E"
Representations and Warranties

[*Note:* Please fill in blanks.]

1. **Representations and Warranties of the Company and the Stockholder(s):**

(a) The Company is a valid corporation under the laws of the State of _____ , is in good standing, and is authorized to carry on its business and enter into this agreement.

(b) The shares owned by the Stockholder(s) who are signing this agreement constitute one hundred percent (100%) of the issued and outstanding shares of the Company, and there are no agreements in existence other than this one that would result in more shares being issued.

(c) The Company, its officers, directors, and shareholders have taken all action necessary to authorize this agreement and the sale of shares by the Company to the Investor. No one else's consent to this agreement or sale of shares is required.

2. **Representations and Warranties of the Investor:**

(a) If the Investor is a corporation: (i) the Investor is a valid corporation under the laws of the State of _____ and is authorized to enter into this agreement, and (ii) the Investor, its officers, directors, and shareholders have taken all action necessary to authorize this agreement and the purchase of shares from the Company, and no other consent to this agreement or purchase is required.

(b) Investor has received all the information regarding the Company, its present and prospective business, assets, liabilities, and financial condition, that it considers necessary or appropriate for deciding whether or not to buy shares from the Company and has had ample opportunity to ask questions and receive answers from the Company and its officers and to obtain any documents requested in order to supplement or verify any of the information supplied.

(c) Investor has experience in investing in companies in the developmental stage, such as the Company, and acknowledges that is able to fend for itself and to assess the economic risk of this purchase, recognizes that this investment involves a high degree of risk and may result in a loss of the entire investment, and has such knowledge and experience in financial and business matters that it can be assumed to be capable of evaluating the merits and risks of this investment and/or protecting its interests in such an investment. Investor is an "accredited investor" as that term is defined in the regulations under Rule 501 of Regulation D of the Securities Exchange Act of 1934, as amended and in the relevant state securities statute and, in the event of inconsistent definitions, whichever definition provides a greater level of sophistication and economic well being.

(d) Investor understands that the shares of stock it is purchasing are and will be characterized as "restricted securities" under the Securities Act of 1933, as amended, because they are being acquired from the Company in a transaction not involving a public offering and that under that Act the stock may be resold without registration only in certain very limited circumstances. Investor understands that subsequent sales of the stock may be subject to federal and/or state restrictions.

EXHIBIT "F"

Legal Opinions

Opinions of Counsel to the Company

(a) The obligation of Investor to purchase shares from the Company is subject, unless waived by placing a check mark or an "x" in this space _____, to the receipt by the Investor of an opinion of counsel for the Company to the following effect:

(i) The Company is validly existing and in good standing under the laws of the State of _____ [*insert state of incorporation*] and has the requisite corporate power and authority to conduct its business.

(ii) The Company has the requisite corporate power and authority to execute, deliver, and perform this Agreement. This agreement has been duly and validly authorized by the Company and duly executed and delivered by an authorized officer of the Company.

(iii) The certificate(s) representing the shares being purchased by the Investor is in due and proper form and has been duly and validly executed by the Company and, upon payment therefor and issuance in accordance with this Agreement, will be duly authorized, validly issued, fully paid, and nonassessable.

Opinion of Counsel to the Investor

(b) If the Investor is a corporation, the obligation of the Company to sell shares to the Investor is subject, unless waived by placing a check mark or an "x" in this space _____, to the receipt by the Company of an opinion of counsel for Investor to the following effect:

(i) The Investor is validly existing and in good standing under the laws of the State of _____ [*insert state of incorporation*] and has the requisite corporate power and authority to conduct its business.

(ii) The Investor has the requisite corporate power and authority to execute, deliver, and perform this Agreement. This agreement has been duly and validly authorized by the Investor and duly executed and delivered by an authorized officer of the Investor.

EXHIBIT "G"

Legends

The certificate representing the shares being purchased by the Investor shall (i) until such time as the same is no longer required under applicable requirements of the Securities Act of 1933, as amended, and the rules and regulations thereunder, contain a legend substantially in the form of subsection (a) below and (ii) until such time as such shares are no longer subject to the restrictions on transfer contained in Sections IV of this Agreement, contain a legend substantially in the form of subsection (b) below (in addition to any legend required under applicable state securities laws):

(a) "THE SECURITIES REPRESENTED HEREBY HAVE NOT BEEN REGISTERED UNDER THE SECURITIES ACT OF 1933, AS AMENDED (THE "ACT"), OR UNDER THE SECURITIES LAWS OF ANY STATES. THESE SECURITIES ARE SUBJECT TO RESTRICTIONS ON TRANSFERABILITY AND RESALE AND MAY NOT BE TRANSFERRED OR RESOLD EXCEPT AS PERMITTED UNDER THE ACT AND THE APPLICABLE STATE SECURITIES LAWS, PURSUANT TO REGISTRATION OR EXEMPTION THEREFROM. THE HOLDER OF THE SECURITIES REPRESENTED HEREBY SHOULD BE AWARE THAT IT MAY BE REQUIRED TO BEAR THE FINANCIAL RISKS OF THIS INVESTMENT FOR AN INDEFINITE PERIOD OF TIME. THE ISSUER OF THESE SECURITIES MAY REQUIRE AN OPINION OF COUNSEL IN FORM AND SUBSTANCE SATISFACTORY TO THE ISSUER TO THE EFFECT THAT ANY PROPOSED TRANSFER OR RESALE IS IN COMPLIANCE WITH THE ACT AND ANY APPLICABLE STATE SECURITIES LAWS."

(b) "THE SECURITIES REPRESENTED BY THIS CERTIFICATE ARE SUBJECT TO RESTRICTIONS ON TRANSFER AND A RIGHT OF FIRST REFUSAL, AS SET FORTH IN AN AGREEMENT DATED _____, AMONG _____ [*Company*], _____ [*Investor(s)*] and _____ [*Stockholder(s)*]. A COPY OF SUCH AGREEMENT MAY BE OBTAINED AT NO COST BY WRITTEN REQUEST MADE BY THE HOLDER OF RECORD OF THIS CERTIFICATE TO THE SECRETARY OF _____ [*Company*] AT ITS PRINCIPAL EXECUTIVE OFFICES."

EXHIBIT "H"

Other Provisions

[*Note:* Please fill in blanks.]

(a) Nothing in this Agreement, express or implied, is intended to confer upon any party other than the parties hereto or their respective successors and assigns any rights, remedies, obligations, or liabilities under or by reason of this Agreement, except as expressly provided in this Agreement.

(b) This Agreement shall be construed and enforced in accordance with, and governed by, the laws of the State of_____, [*insert state in which the principal office of the company is located*] excluding that body of law applicable to conflicts of law.

(c) Unless otherwise provided, any notice required or permitted under this Agreement shall be given in writing and shall be deemed effectively given upon personal delivery to the party to be notified, upon two business days after delivery to a recognized overnight courier service, or upon five business days after deposit in the United States mail, by registered or certified mail, postage prepaid and addressed to the party to be notified at the address indicated for such party on the signature page hereof, or at such other address as such party may designate by ten days' advance written notice to the other parties.

(d) If one or more provisions of this Agreement are held to be unenforceable under applicable law, such provision shall be excluded from this Agreement and the balance of this Agreement shall be interpreted as if such provision were so excluded and shall be enforceable in accordance with its terms.

(e) This Agreement constitutes the entire agreement of the parties concerning the subject matter hereof and supersedes all prior negotiations and undertakings.

The Angel Capital Electronic Network (ACE-*Net*) is a nationwide Internet-based listing service that provides information to angel investors on small, dynamic, growing businesses seeking $250,000 to $5 million in equity financing. ACE-*Net* is a public/private initiative sponsored by the Office of Advocacy of the U.S. Small Business Administration and nine non-profit entrepreneurship centers located throughout the nation. ACE-*Net* was announced by the President of the United States in October 1996. It is a major effort by the Office of Advocacy to start systematizing, on a nationwide basis, and expanding information available to investors on firms seeking equity financing. Once fully operational, ACE-*Net* will be run as a private, not-for-profit organization.

For further information about ACE-*Net*, contact the U.S. Small Business Adminstration's Office of Advocacy at 409 Third Street S.W., Washington, DC 20416, or visit the ACE-*Net* home page on the World Wide Web at *https://ace-net.sr.unh.edu*.

6

North Florida Technology Innovation Corporation of Gainesville

Client Agreements

This section of the appendix includes two client agreements, a one-page version and a considerably longer full-text version. The one-page document is used for clients with whom incubator staff doesn't yet have enough information to draft a full-fledged service agreement. NFTIC uses the document to establish the initial working relationship and drafts a service agreement down the line when the companies needs are better understood.

The longer agreement is the full legal document that NFTIC put together when it first opened. Drafted by a local law firm, the agreement is "loaded with legaleze," says director Larry Albertson, who has discovered that start-up companies find it very intimidating. "We desperately need to get a new document drafted that includes more lay terminology and fewer restrictions and conditions." Although Albertson agrees that the agreement NFTIC ultimately adopts must be substantial enough to give both sides protection, he would like to see the final instrument fall somewhere in between the one-pager and the long version.

The long version does provide an encyclopedic look at the various clauses and conditions that such an agreement can contain. As such, it can serve as a reference document for making certain that all areas important to an incubator and client companies are addressed.

Services Proposals

The Services Proposals here are for three different companies. The differences among them demonstrate that it's impossible to develop a boilerplate service proposal that will work for all companies.

NFTIC-GNV / Client Agreement

AGREEMENT, is made and entered into this ___ day of _____ 19___, by and between the North ... la Technology Innovation Corporation of ...sville, ("NFTIC-GNV") and
_____.
ent")

...ONSIDERATION of the mutual promises herein, ...C-GNV and Client agree as follows:

...NFTIC-GNV Services. a. NFTIC-GNV shall ...de business consultation and assistance services ...ient according to the attached Services Proposal in ...ection with reviewing Client's business plan and ...relevant aspects of Client's business venture.

b. NFTIC-GNV's average charge for services of ...ype contemplated herein is $55.00 per hour. ...ever, NFTIC-GNV HEREBY WAIVES ITS ...NDARD CHARGE FOR THE AMOUNT OF ...VICES REFERRED TO IN PARAGRAPH 1 (a) ...) WILL CHARGE INSTEAD _____
_____.
...e event Client authorizes additional services by ...IC-GNV, Client shall pay NFTIC-GNV its ...cable standard charge for such services and ...burse NFTIC-GNV for any out-of-pocket ...nses incurred in connection therewith.

c. NFTIC-GNV makes no representations or ...anties, expressed or implied, that NFTIC-GNV's ...ces will result in or cause Client's business ...ure to succeed or achieve any specific objectives. ...t has no duty to comply with or follow any advice ...commendations given by NFTIC-GNV and Client ...retain full right and authority to conduct its ...ness in accordance with its own judgment. Subject ...aragraph 2, NFTIC-GNV shall not be restricted by ...Agreement from providing consultation, advice, ...services to other persons or entities engaged in ...lar or competitive businesses as Client's business.

...onfidentiality. Each party shall, and shall require ...lirectors, officers, employees, and agents to, use ...best efforts to keep confidential any information ...otherwise generally available to the public that it ...receive from the other disclosing party as a result ...r in connection with this Agreement regarding the ...ness and affairs of the disclosing party and the ...iving party shall not use and shall use its best ...rts not to disclose or permit any use or disclosure ...eof without the disclosing party's written consent, ...ept as follows: (i) any disclosure required by ...licable law or regulation or by a court or ...ernmental authority acting within its jurisdiction; or

(ii) any use or disclosure of information that was (A) already known to or in the possession of the receiving party at the time of receipt from the disclosing party, (B) in the public domain without disclosure by the receiving party, or (C) obtained by the receiving party from an independent source or otherwise developed independently by the receiving party.

3. Proprietary Rights. Client shall retain ownership of, and this Agreement shall not grant to NFTIC-GNV any license to or other rights in, any patents, copyrights or other intellectual property or propriety rights of Client.

4. Indemnification. Except to the extent resulting solely from the gross negligence, recklessness, willful or intentional misrepresentation, misconduct, or fraud or violation of law by NFTIC-GNV or its directors, officers, employees, or agents, Client hereby indemnifies and shall defend and hold harmless NFTIC-GNV and its directors, officers, employees, and agents from and against any and all claims, actions, suits, proceedings, losses, damages, liabilities, costs, fees, or expenses, joint or several (including without limitation reasonable attorney's fees), arising or resulting from or in connection with (i) NFTIC-GNV's Services, or (ii) any negligence, gross negligence, recklessness, willful or intentional misrepresentation, misconduct or fraud or violation of law by Client or its directors, officers, employees, agents or shareholders.

5. Term. The term of this Agreement is for one year from the date first above written; provided, that either party may terminate this Agreement at any time by notifying the other party in writing. The provisions of paragraphs 2 and 4 shall survive an expiration or termination of this Agreement.

IN WITNESS WHEREOF, the parties hereto have duly executed and delivered this Agreement effective as of the date first above written.

North Florida Technology Innovation Corporation of Gainesville
by_____ date:_____

Name:
Title:

Client:
_____.
by_____ date:_____

Name:
Title:

CLIENT AGREEMENT

**NORTH FLORIDA TECHNOLOGY INNOVATION CORPORATION
OF GAINESVILLE**
One Progress Boulevard, Box 7
Alachua, Florida 32615
Telephone: (904) 462-0498
Telecopier: (904) 462-5261

TERM SHEET

Client: _____
_____
_____

Telephone No.: _____
Telecopier No.: _____

Legal Structure:

State of incorporation: _____
S Election? _____
Equity capitalization:

Class	Par Value	No. Shs. Authorized	No. Shs. Outstanding	No. Shs. in Treasury or Reserved	No. Share-holders

	Name	No. Shs. Owned*	Class	Percentage**
Shareholders:	_____	_____	_____	_____
	_____	_____	_____	_____
	_____	_____	_____	_____
	_____	_____	_____	_____
	Total	_____		_____

* Identify to NFTIC in writing any liens, security interests, pledges, charges, encumbrances, shareholders' agreements or voting trusts.

** Based on number of shares issued and outstanding.

Schedules (check all that apply and attach):

        _____ 1 NFTIC Portion of Client's Revenues
        _____ 2 NFTIC Shares
        _____ 3 Client's Revocation of S Election; NFTIC Shares
        _____ 4 NFTIC Option to Sell NFTIC Shares
        _____ 5 NFTIC Right of First Refusal to Participate in Sale
        _____ 6 Termination by Client's Purchase of NFTIC Shares

Addenda (list any that apply and attach):

Effective Date: _____

        This Client Agreement (the "Agreement") is entered into and is effective as of the Effective Date indicated above by and among North Florida Technology Innovation Corporation of Gainesville, a Florida not-for-profit corporation ("NFTIC"), and the Client and its Shareholders indicated above. This Agreement consists of this Term Sheet, the Standard Terms and Conditions attached hereto, the Schedules designated above as applicable to this Agreement and attached hereto and any Addenda designated above as applicable to this Agreement and attached hereto, all of which are hereby incorporated by reference and made a part of this Agreement and together constitute one and the same agreement among the parties hereto.

Signatures:

        IN WITNESS WHEREOF, the parties have duly executed and delivered this Agreement (by their duly authorized representatives, in the case of Client and NFTIC) as of the Effective Date indicated above.

THIS CONTRACT CONTAINS A BINDING ARBITRATION PROVISION WHICH MAY BE ENFORCED BY THE PARTIES.

North Florida Technology Innova-   Client:_____
tion Corporation of Gainesville

By:_____   By:_____
   Name:_____   Name:_____
   Title:_____   Title:_____

                                         Shareholders:

                                         _____

                                         _____

THE STANDARD TERMS AND CONDITIONS ATTACHED HERETO, TOGETHER WITH ANY SCHEDULES AND ADDENDA DESIGNATED HEREIN AS APPLICABLE AND ATTACHED HERETO, ARE A PART OF THIS AGREEMENT.

STANDARD TERMS AND CONDITIONS

These Standard Terms and Conditions are a part of the Term Sheet to which they are attached and have been incorporated therein by reference together with any applicable Schedules and Addenda. Capitalized terms used in these Standard Terms and Conditions and not otherwise defined herein shall have the respective meanings given to such terms in the Term Sheet. Capitalized terms used in this Agreement shall have the respective meanings given to such terms in these Standard Terms and Conditions.

1. <u>NFTIC Services</u>. NFTIC shall provide the services described below in Section 1(a) to Client, subject to the disclaimers described below in Section 1(b), as follows:

(a) *Services*. The parties acknowledge that, prior to the date hereof, NFTIC has consulted with Client and provided Client with good and valuable services, including (among other things) advice as to Client's organizational structure, business strategies and business location. In addition, during the term of this Agreement, NFTIC shall use reasonable efforts to continue to provide certain services to Client, as NFTIC and Client shall mutually determine from time to time, including, without limitation, technical and scientific advice regarding Client's product(s), consultation and advice regarding financial matters, marketing, organizational structure and business plan development and implementation, and serving as an information resource regarding financing needs and competing and complimentary businesses and services ("NFTIC Services").

(b) *Disclaimers*. NFTIC makes no representations or warranties, express or implied, to Client or the Shareholders with regard to the NFTIC Services or that the NFTIC Services will result in or cause Client's business venture to succeed or achieve any specific objectives. Client has no duty to comply with or follow any advice or recommendations given by NFTIC and Client shall retain full right and authority (subject only to NFTIC's rights as a shareholder of Client, if applicable) to conduct its business in accordance with its own judgment. Subject to Section 4, NFTIC shall not be restricted by this Agreement from providing consultation, advice and services to other persons or entities engaged in similar or competitive businesses as Client's business. In no instance shall NFTIC be deemed to have any fiduciary or other similar duties or obligations to Client or the Shareholders, nor shall NFTIC be deemed to have any implied duties pursuant to this Agreement. Further, all parties acknowledge that none of NFTIC or its directors, officers, employees or agents is a person that controls, is controlled by or is under common control with Client for any purposes, including without limitation for purposes of the Securities Act of 1933, as amended, and the regulations thereunder. No third party is an intended beneficiary of this Agreement.

2. <u>Consideration to NFTIC</u>. In consideration of the NFTIC Services provided or to be provided to Client pursuant to this Agreement, Client hereby agrees (i) to pay to NFTIC the amounts required by Schedule 1, if designated on the Term Sheet as applicable to this Agreement, and (ii) either (a) to issue to NFTIC the shares of Client's capital stock required by Schedule 2, if designated on the Term Sheet as applicable to this Agreement, or (b) if Client is an S corporation, to revoke its S election on or before the date that is two (2) years after the Effective Date of this Agreement and issue to NFTIC the shares of Client's capital stock immediately after such revocation required by Schedule 3, if designated on the Term Sheet as applicable to this Agreement. In further consideration of the NFTIC Services provided or to be provided to Client pursuant to this Agreement, Client hereby grants to NFTIC the rights set forth in Schedules 4 and 5, if designated on the Term Sheet as applicable to this Agreement. All shares of Client's capital stock issued to NFTIC pursuant to any provisions of this Agreement ("NFTIC Shares") shall be subject to Client's rights set forth in Schedule 6, if designated on the Term Sheet as applicable to this Agreement.

3. <u>Client's Covenants, Representations and Warranties</u>. Client hereby covenants with and represents and warrants to NFTIC as follows:

(a) *Incorporation*. Client has been duly incorporated and organized, is validly existing as a corporation under the laws of the state of its incorporation indicated on the Term Sheet (the "Domestic State") and its status is active, and Client has the full right, power and authority to own, lease, license and use its properties and assets, to carry on its business as now conducted or contemplated and to enter into, execute, deliver and perform this Agreement. If Client's Domestic State is not Florida, then Client is duly qualified and to conduct business in the State of Florida as a foreign corporation and its status is active.

(b) *Authorization*. All necessary proceedings and consents, corporate or otherwise, have been duly taken or obtained to authorize the execution, delivery and performance of this Agreement by Client; no consent, authorization, order, license, certificate or permit of or from, or declaration or filing with, any governmental authority, court or other tribunal is required for Client to execute, deliver and perform this Agreement; and this Agreement has been duly authorized, executed and delivered by Client, constitutes the legal, valid and binding obligation of Client and is enforceable against Client in accordance with its terms.

(c) *Execution*. The execution, delivery and performance of this Agreement by Client will not violate, conflict with or result in the breach of or (with or without the giving of notice or the passage of time or both) entitle any party to terminate or declare a default under any provision of any indenture, loan, agreement or other instrument to which Client is a party or by which its properties or assets are bound; and no litigation, arbitration, governmental or other proceeding or investigation is pending or, to Client's or the Shareholders' knowledge, threatened with respect to Client or its properties, assets or business or that would interfere with Client's execution, delivery or performance of this Agreement.

(d) *Capitalization*. The authorized and outstanding capital stock of Client (before giving effect to the issuance of any NFTIC Shares pursuant to Schedules 2 or 3, if applicable) is as indicated on the Term Sheet, with the number of shares held in treasury and the number of shares reserved for or subject to issuance pursuant to agreement, option, warrant, conversion, privilege or other similar rights also as indicated on the Term Sheet; and all the outstanding shares of Client's capital stock are validly authorized and issued, fully paid and nonassessable and all such shares (before giving effect to the issuance of any NFTIC Shares pursuant to Schedules 2 or 3, if applicable) are owned of record by the Shareholders.

(e) *NFTIC Shares*. When any NFTIC Shares are issued to NFTIC pursuant to Schedules 2 or 3, if applicable, (i) such NFTIC Shares will be evidenced by certificates properly completed in NFTIC's name and duly executed and delivered to NFTIC, (ii) such NFTIC Shares will be validly authorized and issued, fully paid and nonassessable, and (iii) the offer, issue and sale of such NFTIC Shares to NFTIC will have been effected in a manner that complies with or is exempt from the registration requirements of the Securities Act of 1933, as amended, and applicable state securities laws and in compliance with the requirements of such exemptions. Client shall, upon reasonable request by NFTIC, provide NFTIC with reasonable evidence that the requirements of this Section 3(e) have been satisfied.

(f) *Additional Documents*. Concurrently with entering into this Agreement, Client shall provide NFTIC with the following documents: (i) Client's certificate or articles of incorporation and all amendments thereto, certified as of a recent date by the secretary of state of the Domestic State; (ii) a certificate as of a recent date by the secretary of state of the Domestic State as to Client's active status as a corporation in the Domestic State; (iii) if Client's Domestic State is not Florida, a certificate as of a recent date by the Secretary of State of Florida as to Client's qualification and active status to conduct business in Florida as a foreign corporation; (iv) Client's bylaws and all amendments thereto, certified as of the date hereof by Client's corporate secretary; (v) resolutions of Client's board of directors approving and authorizing the execution, delivery and performance of this Agreement and the transactions contemplated herein, certified as of the date hereof by Client's corporate secretary; and (vi) a certificate by Client's corporate secretary as of the date hereof as to (A) no further amendments to Client's certificate or articles of incorporation having been adopted or approved and all required corporate filings with and reports to the secretary of state of the Domestic State having been made, (B) no resolutions for the merger, consolidation or dissolution or the sale of all or substantially all of the assets of Client having been adopted or approved, and (C) the due election and qualification, incumbency and genuine signatures of Client's officers. Client shall use its best efforts to maintain its active status referred to in Clauses (ii) and (iii) of this Section 3(f). (The matters referred to in Clauses (iv), (v) and (vi) may be combined into a single document, the form for which is available from NFTIC.)

(g) *No Sale of Assets*. For purposes of protecting NFTIC's rights under Schedules 1, 2, 3, 4 and 5, if applicable, Client shall not, without NFTIC's prior consent in each instance, sell, transfer, assign, pledge, encumber or otherwise dispose of (or enter into any commitment or agreement for such purpose) all or substantially all of or any substantial portion of Client's property or assets (real, personal, tangible, intangible or other type) except for (i) transactions in the ordinary course of Client's business, and (ii) liens to secure the purchase price of property or assets at the time acquired by Client.

(h) *Financial Statements, Books and Records*. Any financial statements of Client or the Shareholders previously provided to NFTIC have been, and any hereafter provided to NFTIC shall be, true, complete and accurate in all material respects and prepared in accordance with generally accepted accounting principles consistently applied. Client shall maintain true, complete and accurate books and records of its business and financial affairs, in accordance with sound business practices and generally accepted accounting principles consistently applied, and shall accurately prepare and timely file any federal, state and local income and other tax returns and reports accompanied by full payment of all taxes then owing by Client. Client shall provide NFTIC with Client's regular financial statements (at least quarterly) and copies of all Client's tax returns promptly when available and otherwise upon NFTIC's reasonable request. In addition, NFTIC shall have the right to inspect and audit Client's books and records and business facilities and operations from time to time upon reasonable prior notice.

Client Obligations. NFTIC may, without notice to the Shareholders, amend, modify, extend or renew the Client Obligations or compromise or forebear from enforcing payment or performance of all or any part of the Client Obligations without affecting the Shareholders' obligations hereunder. The Shareholders shall reimburse NFTIC, promptly upon request, for any and all fees, costs and expenses (including without limitation reasonable attorneys' fees) incurred in connection with enforcing this Agreement, Client Obligations or the Shareholders' guaranty thereof.

(b) *Acknowledgments and Representations*. The Shareholders acknowledge that: (i) the Shareholders will receive a benefit as a result of NFTIC entering into this Agreement and providing NFTIC Services to Client, (ii) but for the Shareholders' guaranty in Section 5(a), NFTIC would be unwilling to enter into this Agreement and provide NFTIC Services to Client, and (iii) the Shareholders' guaranty in Section 5(a) is given as an inducement for NFTIC to enter into this Agreement and provide NFTIC Services to Client. The Shareholders further represent that (A) this Agreement has been duly executed and delivered by the Shareholders, constitutes the legal, valid and binding obligations of the Shareholders and is enforceable against the Shareholders in accordance with its terms, and (B) all outstanding shares of Client's capital stock (before giving effect to the issuance of any NFTIC Shares pursuant to Schedules 2 and 3, if applicable) are owned by the Shareholders free and clear of all liens, security interests, pledges, charges, encumbrances, shareholders' agreements and voting trusts, except any identified to NFTIC in writing pursuant to the Term Sheet. The Shareholders' guaranty in Section 5(a) shall survive notwithstanding any transfer of their ownership interest in Client or other change in their relationship to Client.

6. <u>Indemnification</u>. Except to the extent resulting solely from the gross negligence, recklessness, willful or intentional misrepresentation, misconduct or fraud or violation of law by NFTIC, or its directors, officers, employees or agents, Client hereby indemnifies and shall defend and hold harmless NFTIC and its directors, officers, employees and agents from and against any and all claims, actions, suits, proceedings, losses, damages, liabilities, costs, fees or expenses, joint or several (including without limitation reasonable attorneys' fees), arising or resulting from or in connection with (i) NFTIC Services, (ii) any breach, default or violation under or with respect to any of Client's or the Shareholders' duties, obligations, representations, warranties or covenants contained in this Agreement, (iii) any negligence, gross negligence, recklessness, willful or intentional misrepresentation, misconduct or fraud or violation of law by Client, its directors, officers, employees or agents or the Shareholders, or (iv) any actual or alleged infringement or misappropriation by Client, the

(i) *Legal Compliance*. Client shall at all times comply with all federal, state and local laws, rules, regulations and ordinances applicable to Client's properties, assets and business and shall, upon reasonable request by NFTIC, provide NFTIC with reasonable evidence of such compliance.

(j) *No NFTIC Duties*. Notwithstanding NFTIC's right to inspect, audit and obtain evidence of compliance as set forth in this Agreement, NFTIC shall not be responsible for Client's compliance with any laws, rules, regulations or ordinances or for advising Client as to compliance therewith.

4. <u>Confidentiality and Proprietary Rights</u>. Each party shall, and in the case of Client and NFTIC, they shall require their directors, officers, employees and agents to, use their best efforts to keep confidential any information not otherwise generally available to the public that it may receive from the other disclosing party as a result of or in connection with this Agreement regarding the business and affairs of the disclosing party and the receiving party shall not use and shall use its best efforts not to disclose or permit any use or disclosure thereof without the disclosing party's written consent, except as follows: (i) any disclosure required by applicable law or regulation or by a court or governmental authority acting within its jurisdiction; or (ii) any use or disclosure of information that was (A) already known to or in the possession of the receiving party at the time of receipt from the disclosing party, (B) in the public domain without disclosure by the receiving party, or (C) obtained by the receiving party from an independent source or otherwise developed independently by the receiving party. Client shall retain ownership of, and this Agreement shall not grant to NFTIC any license to or other rights with respect to, any patent, trademark, trade name, copyright or other proprietary or confidential information or intellectual property rights owned or licensed by Client or relating to any product or service developed or marketed by Client.

5. <u>Shareholders' Guaranty</u>. The Shareholders guaranty, acknowledge and represent the following matters:

(a) *Guaranty*. The Shareholders jointly and severally hereby absolutely and unconditionally guarantee to NFTIC the full and timely payment and performance by Client of all Client's duties and obligations to NFTIC under this Agreement ("Client Obligations"). The Shareholders hereby waive notice of acceptance of this guaranty and presentment, demand, protest, notice of protest, notice of default or nonpayment and diligence in enforcing any Client Obligations. The Shareholders further waive any right to require that any action be brought first against Client or that the Shareholders be joined in any such action, or that NFTIC proceed first against any security now or hereafter held by NFTIC for the payment or performance of any

Shareholders or any product or service developed or marketed by Client of any patent, trademark, trade name, copyright or other proprietary or intellectual property right of any person or entity. Upon notice from NFTIC, Client shall defend NFTIC in any claim, action, suit or proceeding described above or any threat thereof and shall promptly assume and thereafter diligently prosecute the defense thereof at Client's cost and expense, using counsel who shall be subject to NFTIC's approval (which approval may be reasonably withdrawn at any time). NFTIC shall be entitled to engage separate counsel and participate in such defense; provided, that the fees, costs and expenses of such separate counsel shall be paid by NFTIC unless the interests of Client and the interests of NFTIC are in conflict so that they cannot be adequately represented by the same counsel, in which event the fees, costs and expenses of such separate counsel shall be paid by Client. Client shall not settle any such claim, action, suit or proceeding or threat thereof without the prior written consent of NFTIC, which consent may be withheld in NFTIC's sole discretion if such settlement would require the expenditure of funds by NFTIC or admit on behalf of or otherwise attribute to NFTIC any fault or misconduct.

7. *Term and Termination*.

(a) *Term*. The term of this Agreement shall commence on the Effective Date of this Agreement indicated on the Term Sheet and shall continue until such date as (i) NFTIC no longer holds any NFTIC Shares and Schedule 3 is not in effect, and (ii) either NFTIC or Client elects to discontinue the service for fee arrangement provided in Schedule 1, if applicable; provided, that this Agreement shall also be subject to termination in the manner permitted by Sections 7(b) and 7(c).

(b) *Default*. If NFTIC or Client (the "Defaulting Party") shall commit any breach, default or violation under or with respect to, or otherwise fail to fully and timely perform or comply with, the Defaulting Party's duties, obligations, representations, warranties or covenants contained in this Agreement, then the other parties (a "Nondefaulting Party") shall have the right to give the Defaulting Party notice of such breach, default, violation or other failure (a "Notice of Default") specifying the nature thereof. If the Defaulting Party does not cure such breach, default, violation or other failure to the Nondefaulting Party's reasonable satisfaction within 30 days from the date such Notice of Default is given, then a Nondefaulting Party shall have the right to terminate this Agreement effective immediately by giving the Defaulting Party notice of such termination not more than 15 days after the expiration of such 30 day cure period. For purposes of this Section 7(b), any breach, default or violation by the Shareholders shall be attributed to and constitute a breach, default or violation by Client.

(c) *Bankruptcy, Insolvency and Change of Control.* Subject to the last sentence of this Section 7(c), this Agreement shall terminate automatically, without any notice or other action by any party being required, effective upon the occurrence of any of the following with respect to NFTIC or Client (the "Terminating Party"): (i) liquidation or dissolution of the Terminating Party or the taking of corporate or other action for the purpose of effecting any of the foregoing, (ii) an assignment for the benefit of the Terminating Party's creditors, the Terminating Party's insolvency or inability to pay debts as they mature, the filing by or against the Terminating Party of a petition, or any answer or consent thereto, seeking liquidation, receivership, reorganization or readjustment of the Terminating Party's property, assets or liabilities under bankruptcy or other insolvency laws, the appointment of a conservator, sequestrator, receiver or trustee for all or substantially all of the Terminating Party's property or assets or liabilities under bankruptcy or other insolvency laws or the taking of corporate or other action for the purpose of effecting any for the foregoing; (iii) a merger, consolidation or other reorganization of the Terminating Party in which the Terminating Party is not the surviving entity; (iv) the sale or other transfer of all or substantially all of the Terminating Party's property or assets or the purchase or other acquisition by any person or group of 50 percent or more of the Terminating Party's outstanding equity interest. Whichever of NFTIC or Client is not the Terminating Party (the "Nonterminating Parties") shall have the right to affirm this Agreement, in which case it shall remain in full force and effect, by so notifying the Terminating Party within 30 days after the Nonterminating Parties first have actual knowledge of any of the foregoing events.

(d) *Survival.* For so long as any NFTIC Shares are held by NFTIC, the provisions of Sections 2, 3(e), 3(g), 3(h), 3(i) and 3(j) and Schedules 1, 2, 3, 4 and 5, if applicable, shall survive, notwithstanding any termination of this Agreement pursuant to Section 7(b) or 7(c). Further, the provisions of Sections 1(b), 4, 5 and 6, together with any provisions of this Agreement affecting the interpretation of any provisions of this Agreement that remain in effect and the accrued obligation hereunder of one party to pay any amounts to the other party, shall survive, notwithstanding any termination of this Agreement.

8. <u>Miscellaneous</u>.

(a) *Interpretation.* The Section numbers and headings preceding text have been inserted for convenient reference only and shall not affect the meaning, construction or effect of this Agreement. Words in the singular include the plural and words in the plural include the singular. Unless otherwise expressly provided, references to Sections are references to Sections of these Standard Terms and Conditions and references to Schedules are references to Schedules applicable to this Agreement. In the event of any conflict between the provisions of the Term Sheet, these Standard Terms and Conditions and any applicable Schedules or Addenda, the conflicting provisions shall be interpreted as controlling in the following priority: (1) any applicable Addenda, (2) any applicable Schedules, (3) the Term Sheet, and (4) these Standard Terms and Conditions.

(b) *Entire Agreement*. This Agreement constitutes the entire understanding of the parties with respect to the subject matter hereof. This Agreement may be executed in multiple counterparts, all of which together shall constitute one and the same agreement. This Agreement may be modified, amended or otherwise altered only in writing signed by all the parties. No party may assign or delegate this Agreement or any rights or duties hereunder without the prior written consent of the other parties. This Agreement shall be binding on, inure to the benefit of and be enforceable by and against the heirs, successors and permitted assigns of each of the parties.

(c) *Remedies*. The delay or failure in the exercise of any right, remedy or power shall not operate as a waiver thereof, nor shall any single or partial exercise or waiver thereof preclude or limit any other or future exercise thereof. Except as otherwise expressly provided herein, rights and remedies provided herein (including without limitation the rights to terminate this Agreement pursuant to Sections 7(b) and 7(c)) are cumulative in addition to any other rights and remedies available herein or at law, in equity or by statute.

(d) *Notices*. All notices, requests, approvals, consents or other communications required or permitted to be delivered herein shall be in writing and shall be sufficient if delivered personally, forwarded by certified U.S. mail with proper postage prepaid and return receipt requested (or by other prepaid commercial delivery service that documents delivery) or transmitted by telecopier with receipt promptly acknowledged by the receiving party, in each case to the party to which directed at its address indicated on the Term Sheet (with communications to the Shareholders directed to Client's address). Unless otherwise expressly provided herein, such communications shall be effective upon delivery to the address of the party to which directed (notwithstanding any acceptance, rejection or acknowledgement of such delivery). Any party may from time to time designate any other address to which such communications shall be sent.

(e) *No Joint Venture*. No party shall hold itself out as an agent, joint venturer or partner of another party or of any entity controlled directly or indirectly by or affiliated with another party.

    (f) *Cooperation*. Each party shall reasonably cooperate with the others, execute and deliver such further documents and instruments and do such further acts as reasonably necessary to give effect to the intent of the parties expressed herein.

    (g) *Severability*. If any court of competent jurisdiction declares invalid or unenforceable any provision of this Agreement, then such invalidity or unenforceability shall have no effect on the other provisions hereof, which shall remain valid, binding and enforceable and in full force and effect, and such invalid or unenforceable provision shall be construed in a manner to give the maximum valid and enforceable effect to the intent of the parties expressed therein.

    (h) *Florida Law*. This Agreement shall be governed by and construed in accordance with the laws of the State of Florida, without regard to its principles of conflicts of laws.

    (i) Waiver of Right to Jury Trial. The parties to this Agreement do hereby waive any right to a trial by jury, to the extent permitted by law, in any action, proceeding, or counterclaim brought by any party against the other on any matters whatsoever arising out of or in any way connected with this Agreement.

SCHEDULE 1

NFTIC's Portion of Client's Revenues

This Schedule 1 is a part of the Term Sheet to which it is attached and has been incorporated therein by reference together with the Standard Terms and Conditions, any other applicable Schedules and any applicable Addenda.

Client shall pay to NFTIC the greater of (a) the respective percentages of Client's Revenues (as defined below) corresponding to the respective amounts of Revenues earned by Client in each of its fiscal years (or portion thereof) in accordance with the schedule set forth below, or (b) an annual minimum in the amount set forth below for each such fiscal year (with a minimum of one-fourth thereof payable each quarter), on the following terms and conditions:

1. Payments to NFTIC shall be due and payable within 15 days after the close of each of the first three quarters and within 30 days after the close of the last quarter in Client's fiscal year with respect to the Revenues received by Client during such quarter. Any amount not paid when due shall bear interest at the fixed rate of 10% per annum (without compounding) until paid, but without limiting NFTIC's rights under Section 7(b) of the Agreement.

2. Each payment shall be accompanied by a statement, signed by Client's chief financial officer, setting forth Client's calculation of such payment in reasonable detail. All amounts paid hereunder shall be subject to adjustment at the time the payment is due for the last quarter in Client's fiscal year based on Client's annual financial statements for such year. Client's obligations under this Schedule 1 shall begin with the first full quarter that begins on or after the Effective Date of this Agreement, but shall be calculated with respect to the Revenues for Client's full fiscal year in which such quarter in included.

3. For purposes of this Schedule 1, "Revenues" means Client's gross annual revenues, net of returns, rebates and allowances, calculated on the same basis as calculated for Client's federal income tax return.

4. Upon any termination of this Schedule 1, amounts payable to NFTIC hereunder with respect to the quarter in which such termination occurs shall be prorated, based on the number of days in such quarter and the number of days thereof through the effective date of termination.

Regular Fee Schedule:

NFTIC Percentage	Annual Revenues ($) More than	Up to
_____ %	$0 (zero)	$_____ (_____)
_____ %	$_____ (_____)	$_____ (_____)
_____ %	$_____ (_____)	$_____ (_____)
_____ %	$_____ (_____)	$_____ (_____)

No percentage paid on revenues in excess of $_____ (_____)
Annual Minimum: $_____ (_____) billed $_____ (_____) per quarter

Alternative Fee Schedule:

During any period in which NFTIC does not hold any of the capital stock of Client pursuant to Schedules 2 or 3, the following schedule shall apply:

NFTIC Percentage	Annual Revenues ($) More than	Up to
_____ %	$0 (zero)	$_____ (_____)
_____ %	$_____ (_____)	$_____ (_____)
_____ %	$_____ (_____)	$_____ (_____)
_____ %	$_____ (_____)	$_____ (_____)

No percentage paid on revenues in excess of $_____ (_____)
Annual Minimum: $_____ (_____) billed $_____ (_____) per quarter

Initials: _____ Client
          _____ NFTIC

SCHEDULE 2

NFTIC Shares

This Schedule 2 is a part of the Term Sheet to which it is attached and has been incorporated therein by reference together with the Standard Terms and Conditions, any other applicable Schedules and any applicable Addenda.

In consideration of the NFTIC Services provided or to be provided to Client pursuant to this Agreement, within 30 days after the Effective Date of this Agreement, Client shall issue to NFTIC a number of shares of capital stock of Client so that, after giving effect to such issuance, NFTIC shall own the NFTIC Percentage indicated below as to each class of capital stock of Client then outstanding or subject to issuance by Client pursuant to any agreement, option, warrant, conversion, privilege or other similar rights. In addition, in the event Client undertakes to issue any additional shares of capital stock or enter into or grant any agreement, option, warrant, conversion, privilege or other similar rights with respect thereto at any time while holds any shares of Client's capital stock issued pursuant to any provisions of this Agreement, and notwithstanding any limitations on preemptive rights contained in Client's articles of incorporation, Client hereby grants to NFTIC the preemptive right to acquire a number of additional shares of Client's capital stock necessary to maintain such NFTIC Percentage ownership of each class of Client's capital stock, on the same terms as Client undertakes to issue such additional shares or enter into or grant such rights with respect thereto.

NFTIC Percentage: _____ % (_____ percent)

Initials: _____ Client
 _____ NFTIC

SCHEDULE 3

Client's Revocation of S Election; NFTIC Shares

This Schedule 3 is a part of the Term Sheet to which it is attached and has been incorporated therein by reference together with the Standard Terms and Conditions, any other applicable Schedules and any applicable Addenda.

In consideration of the NFTIC Services provided or to be provided to Client pursuant to this Agreement, on or before the date that is two (2) years after the Effective Date of this Agreement, the Shareholders shall revoke Client's S election and Client shall immediately thereafter issue to NFTIC a number of shares of capital stock of Client so that, after giving effect to such issuance, NFTIC shall own the NFTIC Percentage indicated below as to each class of capital stock of Client then outstanding or subject to issuance by Client pursuant to any agreement, option, warrant, conversion, privilege or other similar rights. Client shall not issue any shares of capital stock other than to the Shareholders prior to the revocation of its S election and the issuance of capital stock to NFTIC unless such additional shareholder agrees to bound by this Agreement. Each of the certificates representing Client's capital stock outstanding on the Effective Date of this Agreement and thereafter issued before Client issues stock to NFTIC shall contain a restrictive legend describing the restrictions on the capital stock imposed by this Schedule 3 (which description may be by reference to this Agreement). In addition, in the event Client undertakes to issue any additional shares of capital stock or enter into or grant any agreement, option, warrant, conversion, privilege or other similar rights with respect thereto at any time while NFTIC hold any shares of Client's capital stock issued pursuant to any provisions of this Agreement, and notwithstanding any limitations on preemptive rights contained in Client's articles of incorporation, Client hereby grants to NFTIC the preemptive right to acquire a number of additional shares of Client's capital stock necessary to maintain such NFTIC Percentage ownership of each class of Client's capital stock, on the same terms as Client undertakes to issue such additional shares or enter into or grant such rights with respect thereto.

NFTIC Percentage: ____% (_____ percent)

Initials: _____ Client
_____ NFTIC

SCHEDULE 4

NFTIC's Option to Sell NFTIC Shares

This Schedule 4 is part of the Term Sheet to which it is attached and has been incorporated therein by reference together with the Standard Terms and Conditions, any other applicable Schedules and any applicable Addenda.

In the event Client attains the performance goal identified below, Client shall promptly notify NFTIC thereof and NFTIC shall have the option, exercisable in NFTIC's sole discretion then or at any time thereafter, to sell all the NFTIC Shares (including any NFTIC Shares transferred pursuant to Section 2) to Client on the following terms and conditions:

1. NFTIC shall notify Client in writing of the exercise of NFTIC's option hereunder. Client shall purchase the NFTIC Shares on a mutually agreeable date not more than 30 days after the date of NFTIC's notice (the "Closing Date").

2. The purchase price for the NFTIC Shares shall be determined using the formula set forth below and shall be payable to NFTIC as follows: one-third in cash on the Closing Date, one-third in cash on the first anniversary of the Closing Date and one-third in cash on the second anniversary of the Closing Date.

3. Any portion of the purchase price not paid on the Closing Date shall bear interest from the Closing Date until the date paid at a fixed rate of interest equal to the prime rate in effect on the business day prior to the Closing Date as published on the Closing Date in the Eastern edition of <u>The Wall Street Journal</u> or such other rate as may be mutually agreeable to the parties. All accrued and unpaid interest shall be paid on each anniversary date of the Closing Date.

4. NFTIC shall have the right to require Client to execute and deliver to NFTIC on the Closing Date (A) a promissory note in the amount of any portion of the purchase price not paid on the Closing Date, (B) a pledge agreement pledging all the NFTIC Shares to NFTIC as security for the promissory note, and (C) such other documents and instruments as may be necessary in NFTIC's judgment to perfect and preserve its security interest in the NFTIC Shares so pledged.

Performance Goal: After-tax net earnings exceed _____ _____ Dollars ($_____) in any one fiscal year.

Purchase Price Formula: Amount equal to the percentage of outstanding Client Shares held by NFTIC at a valuation of _____ (__) times after-tax net earnings.

Initials: _____ Client
          _____ NFTIC

SCHEDULE 5

<u>NFTIC's Right of First Refusal to Participate in Sale</u>

This Schedule 5 is a part of the Term Sheet to which it is attached and has been incorporated therein by reference together with the Standard Terms and Conditions, any other applicable Schedules and any applicable Addenda.

In the event Client or any Shareholder (the "Seller") receives any offer to purchase that it desires to accept or makes any offer to sell with respect to any shares of Client's capital stock (an "Offer"), such Offer must allow the participation rights of NFTIC described below. NFTIC shall have the right to participate in the sale contemplated in the Offer by electing to sell to the proposed purchaser (for the price and upon the terms which such shares are otherwise to be sold) up to the number of shares determined by multiplying the total shares to be purchased by the purchaser pursuant to the Offer by a fraction, the numerator of which is the total shares to be sold by the Seller pursuant to the Offer, and the denominator of which is the shares owned by the Seller and NFTIC; the Seller shall reduce the number of shares it sells pursuant to such Offer by the number of shares NFTIC elects to sell to the purchaser pursuant to this Paragraph.

The following terms and conditions shall apply with respect to any Offer:

1. Client or such Shareholder shall notify NFTIC in writing as to such Offer and the terms thereof, and shall provide NFTIC with a copy of all related documents. NFTIC shall have 30 days after receipt of such notice in which to exercise its right hereunder by giving Client or such Shareholder written notice thereof.

2. If NFTIC exercises its right hereunder, then the sale of the NFTIC Shares (or portion thereof) shall be closed in accordance with the terms of such Offer or on such other terms as may be mutually agreeable to NFTIC, Client or such Shareholder and the purchaser.

3. If NFTIC does not exercise its right hereunder, then Client or such Shareholder shall be permitted to close the transaction in accordance with the terms of such Offer within a reasonable time thereafter; provided, that any material change in the terms of such Offer or delay in closing the transaction shall be deemed to result in a new Offer that is subject to all the provisions of this Schedule 5.

4. NFTIC shall continue to have the rights hereunder notwithstanding any decision by NFTIC not to exercise its rights hereunder with respect to any prior Offer or to exercise its rights hereunder only as to a portion of the NFTIC Shares.

5. For purposes of determining whether an "Offer" has been received or made within the meaning of this Schedule 5, the

terms "purchase" and "sale" shall include (without limitation) any exchange, pledge or other disposition and any contract or commitment therefor. Further, any Offer must reflect a bona fide, arm's length transaction that is binding on the offering party (subject only to the restrictions of this Schedule 5).

Initials: _____ Client
_____ NFTIC

SCHEDULE 6

Termination by Client's Purchase of NFTIC Shares

This Schedule 6 is a part of the Term Sheet to which it is attached and has been incorporated therein by reference together with the Standard Terms and Conditions, any other applicable Schedules and any applicable Addenda.

Client shall have the right, exercisable in Client's sole discretion at any time on or before the expiration of the initial term of this Agreement indicated on the Term Sheet, to terminate this Agreement (including any obligations of Client to pay a portion of its Revenues to NFTIC pursuant to Schedule 1, if applicable) and purchase all the NFTIC Shares by paying to NFTIC the early termination price in cash as determined using the formula set forth below; provided, that Client shall notify NFTIC of its decision to exercise its right hereunder at least 30 days prior to the date thereof, after which notice Client's decision shall be irrevocable.

This Schedule 6 shall terminate upon the expiration of the number of years indicated below after the Effective Date of this Agreement.

Early Termination Price Formula: The amount of _____ Dollars ($_____) or _____ percent (___%) of the market value of such shares as established by a bona fide third party offer for the NFTIC Shares, whichever is greater.

Expiration: _____ (___) years

Initials: _____ Client
         _____ NFTIC

F:\TAX\JDC\20787CS.99C (June 1995)

Services Proposal

NFTIC-GNV proposes to provide the following services to ▇▇▇▇▇▇▇▇▇▇▇▇▇▇ Inc. (LOCI), provided that NFTIC-GNV and LOCI negotiate a final contract (which contract shall include the return to NFTIC-GNV from LOCI for the services provided by NFTIC-GNV) and that such final contract is approved by the NFTIC-GNV and LOCI Boards of Directors.

1. Assist LOCI in implementing a computer based accounting system and establishing internal financial and accounting record-keeping procedures and controls needed to maintain financial and accounting records for LOCI.
   Time: 9 to 12 months

2. Assist in preparing LOCI to source financing, identifying and developing sources of financing to support contract activities and supporting the company through the due diligence process; provided, that in no event shall NFTIC-GNV engage in any selling activities with respect to any securities or take any other action that would require licensure as a securities broker/dealer or an investment advisor.
   Time: 3 to 6 months

3. Assist LOCI in preparing, updating and maintaining a five-year business plan for LOCI's business operations – this includes the basic government contracting business as well as developing a strategy and plans for establishing significant commercial business for the company. The initial business plan should be completed within 9 months
   Time: Ongoing

4. Assist LOCI President, ▇▇▇▇▇▇▇▇▇▇, to develop a succession plan for providing future leadership for the company.
   Time: 12 months

5. Provide guidance on personnel and operations issues as required; assist in identifying appropriate management candidates.
   Time: Ongoing

6. Act as a business advisor to LOCI President, ▇▇▇▇▇▇▇▇▇▇, on all general business matters through regular monthly meetings; perform additional tasks mutually agreed upon by NFTIC-GNV and LOCI over the course of the contract.
   Time: Ongoing

It is understood that NFTIC-GNV's resource expenditure will fluctuate based on the needs and priorities of the tasks identified above. NFTIC-GNV's average monthly resources allocated to LOCI during the first 12 months of this agreement will be 150 hours (necessary to complete the work on the accounting system and the initial business plan); for the second 12 months the allocation will average 100 hours; for the third 12 months the allocation will average 75 hours; and the monthly expenditure thereafter will average 50 hours.

NFTIC-GNV will provide monthly reports for the first year and quarterly reports thereafter delineating the tasks accomplished, the hours expended, and tasks planned for the following period for LOCI's approval.

NFTIC-GNV makes no representations or warranties, express or implied, to ▓▓▓▓▓▓▓ Inc. or its shareholders with regard to the proposed services of NFTIC-GNV or that the proposed services of NFTIC-GNV will result in or cause LOCI's business to succeed or achieve any specific objectives.

▓▓▓▓▓▓▓▓▓▓, President
▓▓▓▓▓▓▓ Inc.

Lawrence P. Albertson, President
NFTIC-GNV

6-3-96
Date

6/3/96
Date

Services Proposal

NFTIC-GNV proposes to provide the following services to ▓▓▓▓▓▓▓▓▓▓, provided that NFTIC-GNV and ▓▓▓▓▓ negotiate a final contract (which contract shall include the return to NFTIC-GNV from ▓▓▓▓▓ for the services provided by NFTIC-GNV) and that such final contract is approved by the NFTIC-GNV and ▓▓▓▓▓▓▓▓ Boards of Directors.

1. Assist ▓▓▓▓▓▓ in developing, expanding and maintaining a five year business plan. Plan will be prepared in two steps and will include full financial projections, manufacturing plans, marketing strategies, funding scenarios, and management/staffing requirements.
   Time: a. Initial Business Plan: Six months
   b. Long-term Business Plan: 24 months

2. Assist ▓▓▓▓▓▓ in preparation for the company to secure financing needed to accommodate projected growth: identify potential sources for funding; support company during the due diligence process; help structure necessary presentations and documentation; provided that in no event shall NFTIC-GNV engage in any selling activities with respect to any securities or take any other action that would require licensure as a security broker/dealer or an investment advisor.
   Time: a. Bridge Funding: Company seeks to raise short-term working capital within 30-60 days
   b. Long-Term Funding: Amount and timing of need to be determined within 12 months

3. Assist in implementation of hardware/software for a computerized accounting system including pricing model; assist in developing appropriate financial controls and training of company personnel.
   Time: 12 months

4. Assist company in identifying and securing appropriate technical and professional resources as necessary to support company growth.
   Time: Ongoing

5. Assist company with relocation/expansion plans at point in time when additional facilities are required.
   Time: During first year of contract

6. Assist in developing a long-term exit strategy for ▓▓▓▓▓ investors (IPO, acquisition, stock repurchase, etc.) including effects of short-term funding activities.
   Time: 24 months

7. Long-term assistance in supplementing managerial requirements, defining management needs, and recruiting appropriate candidates.
   Time: Ongoing

8. Assist in preparation of marketing and public relation materials and help to promote the company in the community (important with regard to financing activities).
   Time: 24 months

9. Perform additional tasks mutually agreed upon by NFTIC-GNV and ▓▓▓▓▓ over the course of the contract.
   Time: Ongoing

It is understood that NFTIC-GNV's resource expenditure will fluctuate based on the need and priorities of the tasks identified above. NFTIC-GNV average monthly resources allocated to ▓▓▓▓▓ during the first 12 months of this agreement will be 100 hours; for the second 12 months the allocation will average 75 hours; and the monthly expenditure thereafter will average 50 hours. NFTIC-GNV will provide quarterly reports delineating the tasks accomplished and the hours expended.

NFTIC-GNV makes no representations or warranties, express or implied, to ▓▓▓▓▓ or its shareholders with regard to the proposed services of NFTIC-GNV or that the proposed services of NFTIC-GNV will result in or cause ▓▓▓▓▓ business to succeed or achieve any specific objectives.

_____   _Lawrence P. Albertson_____
                                          Lawrence P. Albertson, President
                                          NFTIC-GNV

12-16-96   12/16/96
─────────────   ─────────────
Date   Date

Services Proposal

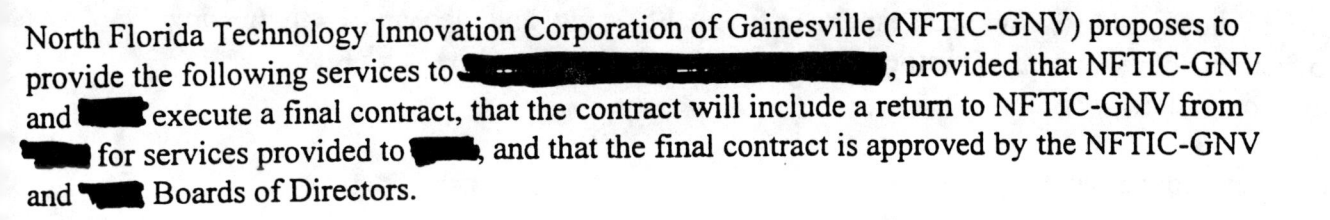

North Florida Technology Innovation Corporation of Gainesville (NFTIC-GNV) proposes to provide the following services to ▓▓▓▓▓▓▓▓▓▓, provided that NFTIC-GNV and ▓▓ execute a final contract, that the contract will include a return to NFTIC-GNV from ▓▓ for services provided to ▓▓, and that the final contract is approved by the NFTIC-GNV and ▓▓ Boards of Directors.

1. Assist ▓▓ in preparing the company to secure adequate initial financing of $250,000 for prototype development and testing, and an additional $250,000 for purchase of manufacturing equipment and working capital (including marketing and product distribution expenses).

   a) Near-term tasks include preparation of an effective investor information package for distribution to prospective investors and identification and qualification of potential investors.

   Time duration: 3 months.

   b) Intermediate-term tasks include assistance with formal presentations to investors and full support during the due diligence and negotiation process.

   Time duration: 6 months

2. Provide comprehensive long-term on-going financial planning and funding assistance for future growth consistent with the business plan and funding needs.

   Time duration: 36 months.

3. Assist ▓▓ in updating its Business Plan, including the development and ongoing maintenance of a long-term Operations Plan.

   Time duration: short-term, 3 months
                       long-term, 36 months

4. Assist ▓▓ with preparing for applications to and approvals from pertinent regulatory and other agencies such as the Occupational Safety and Health Administration (OSHA), the Environment Protection Agency (EPA) and Underwriters Laboratories.

   Time duration: 6 months

▓▓▓▓▓▓▓▓▓▓▓, Proposed Service Agreement, page two

5. Locate and coordinate with local experts in the health, safety and mechanical engineering fields to facilitate development of prototype design features to satisfy OSHA, EPA and mechanical operation criteria.

   Time duration: 3 months

6. Assist ▓▓▓ in preparing for the opportunity to demonstrate its technology at a national trade show in December, 1997. This includes development of trade show booth concept and supporting literature and graphics.

   Time duration: 6 months

7. Perform market research to develop a detailed assessment of competitors and demand for immediate input to the Business Plan and for long-term planning

   Time duration: short-term, 6 months
   long-term, 36 months

8. Assist in the formulation of a comprehensive market strategy to determine target segments, entry tactics and distribution plan and the preparation of a comprehensive marketing plan.

   Time duration: 3 months.

9. Assist in coordinating the design and production of appropriate market communication strategy and materials (*e.g.*, media selection, capabilities brochure, specific product literature, data sheets).

   Time duration: 36 months.

10. Assist ▓▓▓ in locating, qualifying and assembling a professional management team as company growth, size and needs dictate.

   Time duration: 12 months

11. Assist ▓▓▓ with the protection of intellectual property rights, especially in the international market.

   Time duration: 6 months

12. Perform additional tasks mutually agreed upon by NFTIC-GNV and ▓▓▓ during the term of the contract.

   Time duration: 60 months.

Proposed Service Agreement, page three

NFTIC-GNV's resource expenditure will fluctuate based on the needs and priorities of the tasks identified above. The NFTIC-GNV average monthly resources allocated to ▆ will be 100 hours per month during the first 12 months of this agreement, 75 hours per month during the second year, 50 hours per month during the third year, 30 hours per month during the fourth year and 20 hours per month during the fifth year. ▆ and NFTIC-GNV will jointly develop a time line to describe the sequence and initiation dates of the previously-described tasks.

NFTIC-GNV will provide quarterly written reports for the first year and semi-annual reports thereafter delineating the tasks accomplished, the hours expended, and the tasks planned for the following period for ▆ approval.

In no event shall NFTIC-GNV engage in any selling activities with respect to any securities or pursue any other action that would require licensure as a securities broker or dealer or an investment banker.

NFTIC-GNV makes no representations or warranties, express or implied, to ▆ or its shareholders with regard to the proposed services of NFTIC-GNV or that the proposed services of NFTIC-GNV will result in or cause ▆ business to succeed or achieve any specific objectives.

_____, President   _____ Date

_____   _____ Date

Lawrence P. Albertson, President   4/29/97
NFTIC-GNV   Date

Index

A

action plan · 8, 12, 13, 14, 17, 20
additional payments · 32
admissions review committee · 9
affiliate companies · 8
Albertson, Larry · 11, 12, 15, 19, 22, 23, 25, 27, 33, 35
angel investors · 5, 13
authority to exercise agreement · 33

B

balance sheets, reviewing · 34
Battelle · 16
Bendis, Rich · 24, 25, 26, 29, 34, 35
Big Six accounting firms · 29, 41
board of directors · 10, 21, 28, 30, 34, 36
Boulder Technology Incubator (BTI) · 6, 8, 9, 13, 16, 20
Breamer, Dallas · 2, 6, 9, 10, 11, 21, 22, 25, 29, 32, 33, 34
Buehler, Janet · 28
business assistance programs · 1, 4
business assistance services · 6, 33
business incubation programs · 1
business incubators · 1
business plan · 6, 9, 10, 13, 15, 16, 17, 18, 21, 22, 33

C

C corporations · 27, 29
capital networks · 6, 13
Center for Technological Entrepreneurship · 4
common stock · 21, 26, 27
contracts · 3, 8, 9, 10, 12, 17, 19, 20, 22, 24, 25, 28, 29, 31, 32, 33, 34, 35, 36, 39, 43
conversion rate · 32
Coopers & Lybrand L.L.P. · 28

D

Day, David · 26, 36
debenture note · 10, 21, 24, 32
    converting to equity · 10
dilution · 24
Donahue, Jerry · 8, 9, 11, 13, 14, 16, 17, 18, 20, 22, 24, 29, 30, 31, 32, 34, 43
due diligence · 11, 12, 13, 16, 17, 20, 32

E

economic development · 13, 41
employee compensation · 33
equity, amount incubator takes · 2
equity and royalty arrangements
    advantages to companies · 1, 5
    advantages to incubator · 1
    benefits to business assistance programs · 4
    establishing ownership · 40
    risks · 7
    SPEDD · 12
equity arrangement · 2
equity pool · 30
equity position
    buyout · 1
    negotiating · 2
    Tri-Cities Enterprise Association · 2
equity position, effect of amount on investors · 26
exit strategy · 11, 15

F

feasibility studies · 31
financial projections · 15
financial statements, reviewing · 5
first round of financing, how equity/royalty arrangements affect · 5
for-profit incubators · 10, 29, 40
founder's stock · 21, 24

G

Genesis Business Center · v, 1, 5, 7, 10, 13, 15, 21, 29, 34
GENESIS Technology Incubator · 5, 37, 38
gross margins · 11, 15

H

Harrison, Wilson · 36
high-growth companies, · 3

I

incentive plans · 30
incubator closing · 35, 41
incubator services, valuing · 24
incubator, nonprofit
    how equity arrangments affect tax status · 27
insurance · 33
intellectual property · 3, 36, 38
Internal Revenue Service · 28
inventions · 36, 37, 38
investors · 6
investors, linking companies with · 5
InvoTek · 38

J

Jacobs, Harlan · 1, 5, 6, 7, 10, 11, 13, 15, 21, 29, 34

K

Kansas Technology Enterprise Corporation (KTEC) · 24, 25, 26, 29, 34

L

late payment penalties · 32
lease agreement · 38, 39
license fees · 36
liquidating equity or royalty · 15

M

management team · 8, 11, 13, 14, 16, 17
management team, incubator participating in · 17
marketing strategy · 5, 6, 14
Meeder, Bob · 4, 6, 12, 13, 14, 15, 23
mentors · 13
mission, incubator
    SPEDD · 13
mock presentations · 13
monitoring company progress · 5, 8, 34
mutual obligations · 31

N

National Institutes of Health · 38
North Florida Technology Innovation Corporation (NFTIC) · 11, 15, 19, 22, 23, 25, 32, 33, 35

O

offering memorandum · 10
Office for the Advancement of Developing Industries (OADI) · 36
Office for the Advancement of Developing Industries (OADI) incubator · 26
Office of Research Sponsored Programs, University of Arkansas · 38

P

patents · 3, 11, 15, 27, 36, 38, 39
payment schedule · 31
Prism Fiber Optics · 14
private inurement · 28
private investors · 20
private placement memorandum · 17
pro bono professional services · 17
progress reviews · 6
Pruett, Sam · 5, 26, 37, 38, 39
public offerings · 2, 11, 15, 18, 32

R

Rensselaer Polytechnic Institute · 4
rent · 17, 21, 23, 29, 32, 40

restricted legend stock · 24
return on investment
    TEA microequity loan · 24
review committee · 10
review panels · 17
Rice, Mark · 4
right of first refusal · 28
rounds of funding · 13
rounds of investment · 6
royalty arrangements · 3
    time frame · 3, 12
royalty commissions
    percent of sales · 3

S

S corporations · 27
sales projections · 23
screening companies · 8, 12
    Boulder Technology Incubator · 8
    for royalty arrangements · 11
securities attorney · 10, 30
seed capital funds · 29
self-sufficiency, incubator · 40
service agreements · 25
service contract · 22
service schedule · 33
software · 26
SPEDD · 4, 6, 8, 12, 13, 14, 15, 23
step-up company · 12, 14
stock
    use by companies · 1
stock options · 24
stock warrant agreement · 1
stock warrants · 24
Sybert, Ed · 27, 37

T

tax returns · 34
tax status · 19, 27
tax status, 501(c)(3) · 28, 29
TEA microequity fund · 2, 9, 24
technology · 14, 15, 16, 26
terms of obligation · 10
third-party acquisition · 2, 11, 15, 31
time frame for negotiations · 12
time frame, equity/royalty arrangements · 31
time limit, equity/royalty arrangements · 26
Tri-Cities Enterprise Association (TEA) · 2, 6, 9, 10, 21, 24, 29, 32, 33, 34

U

U.S. Department of Energy · 10, 21
UAB Research Foundation · 36
universities, equity/royalty arrangements in · 36
University of Alabama at Birmingham's Research Foundation · 26
University of Arkansas · 5
University of Maryland Technology Advancement Program (TAP) · 2, 27, 37

V

valuation · 2, 10, 20, 21, 22, 34
    how equity/royalty arrangements affect · 5
value of services · 2
venture capitalists · 5, 6, 7, 17